Forty Stories of
Famous Gospel Songs

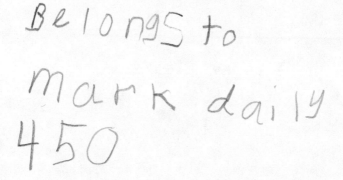

Belongs to
mark daily
450

Forty Stories
of
Famous Gospel Songs

by

Ernest K. Emurian

BAKER BOOK HOUSE

Grand Rapids, Michigan

Library of Congress Catalog Card Number: 59-14830
ISBN: 0-8010-3267-9

PHOTOLITHOPRINTED BY CUSHING - MALLOY, INC.
ANN ARBOR, MICHIGAN, UNITED STATES OF AMERICA

To
The Memory Of
My Two Grandfathers
Ministers And Missionaries
Krikor B. Emurian
and
Harutune S. Jenanyan

PREFACE

Following the injunction of St. Paul in Ephesians 5:18-19, "Be not drunk with wine wherein is excess, but be filled with the Spirit, speaking to yourselves in psalms, hymns and spiritual songs," Christians have used metrical versions of the Old Testament Psalms, as well as their own original hymns (sacred poems addressed to or descriptive of one of the Persons of the Holy Trinity) and spiritual songs (sacred poems descriptive of one's own individual Christian experience) as worthy instruments for the praise of God.

During the years when believers began writing their own hymns, they created only what we know today as the stanzas. Watts and Wesley, Heber and Lyte never made use of what is popularly called a Chorus or Refrain. This device was a purely American invention, designed when the Sunday School movement began to attract thousands of illiterate boys and girls who wanted to take part in congregational singing, but could not because they were unable to read. Hence, those who could read sang the stanzas while those who couldn't memorized the Choruses. In our own day the pendulum has swung to the opposite extreme, and, whereas Watts and Wesley sang stanzas without Choruses, many moderns sing Choruses without any stanzas. The best gospel songs hit a happy medium between these two extremes, using both the stanza and the refrain as a means of instruction, inspiration and mutual edification.

The stories included in this volume should convince the reader that God was just as much at work in the hearts and minds of those consecrated men and women who wrote our finest gospel hymns and songs as He was in the experiences of those poetic giants who fashioned the stately hymns which have become a noble part of our Christian heritage.

I am deeply indebted to everyone who has made this volume possible, especially to those correspondents from far and near who answered my numerous persistent letters of inquiry, and to those relatives and friends of the writers of yesteryear who so graciously complied with my repeated requests for information and historical data, as well as to those who gave me other leads to follow when older trails ended up in dead end streets. As you read these stories, give glory to God, since it was the inspiration of His Spirit brooding across the hearts and minds of many different individuals in various climes and times that gave Christendom these gospel songs, by means of which we are still privileged to exalt the Name of Him Whom we call Our Saviour and Our Lord.

Ernest K. Emurian
Cherrydale United Methodist Church
Arlington, Virginia

INDEX OF COMPOSERS

(Numbers refer to chapters)

CONTENTS

1.

ASLEEP IN JESUS

Margaret MacKay had no more of a morbid pre-occpuation with funerals and cemeteries than did most other normal young women of her day, but she loved to leave the hustle and bustle of the crowded city to find solace and strength in the silence and solemnity of a nearly-forgotten country burying ground.

This feminine fascination for out-of-the-way cemeteries was shared by a large number of sensitive women who enjoyed getting away from home long enough to read some of the curious, serious, humorous, biographical, tragic and ridiculous epitaphs which were inscribed upon many a moss-covered tomb stone in many an out-of-the-way church yard. Few of these pathetic attempts at humor or pathos were worthy of being called poetry by any stretch of the imagination, but they provided recreation and amusement for many women who wanted another excuse for a jaunt in the country on a pleasant spring morning, a warm summer afternoon or a cool evening in the early fall. And Margaret MacKay, who was born a MacKay and married a MacKay and thus was a MacKay all her single and married life, was no exception. Browsing through an old burying ground was to her an interesting and delightful experience, and if she had to raise up a toppled down old stone in one place and dig through the accumulated moss in another, and pull up some vines that had been growing with reckless abandon for many unmolested years in yet another, that, to her, was all part of the pleasure involved in just such a venture into the distant past. These jaunts into the rural areas and these visits to what some cynical scorners called "the marble orchards" of yesteryear, soon convinced the travellers that only a genius could be inspired to pen the immortal words which the English man of letters, Thomas Gray, (1716-1771) wrote, when he gave the world his "Elegy Written in a Country

Churchyard", for the gap between his majestic stanzas and the doggerel which adorned the average tomb stone was practically beyond bridging. A perfect illustration could be found in the violent contrast between Gray's opening stanza, and a typical example of cheap doggerel at its worst. For Gray had begun his poem with these words:

> The Curfew tolls the knell of parting day;
> The lowing herd winds slowly o'er the lea;
> The ploughman homeward plods his weary way
> And leaves the world to darkness and to me.

At the opposite extreme, an unknown poet of the past had expressed his sentiments in this manner:

Here lies my wife, Samantha Proctor; She had a cold and wouldn't doctor;
She couldn't stay; she had to go. Praise God from whom all blessings flow.

It was in 1832 that thirty-year-old Margaret MacKay, the only daughter of Captain Robert MacKay, and a native of Hedgefield, Inverness, Scotland, made her trip to the burying ground of Pennycross Chapel in Devonshire, England, "just a few miles from a crowded seaport town, reached through a succession of lovely green lanes for which that province is so remarkable." The quiet aspect of the site calmed the mind of the young poet with a soothing balm that was almost out-of-this-world in its effect upon her. Soon she was reading the various inscriptions and epitaphs on many of the head and foot-stones, pronouncing the names of the honored dead, and repeating aloud the years of birth and death, and the sentiments, however lofty or lowly, which loved ones had placed there in undecaying stone for future generations to read, remark upon and remember.

Then suddenly she saw the brief statement containing but three words that summed up everything the more voluble writers had attempted to say, but nearly always in vain. For she read this simple inscription carved upon a marble slab at the head of one of the neglected graves: "Sleeping in Jesus".

"That is all that is necessary," she said to herself. "When believers in the Lord die, they go to sleep in Him, and when they

12

awaken over on the other side, they awaken in Him." The more lengthy poems and sentences that she had been reading prior to that dramatic moment faded into insignificance before the magnificence of that simple statement, and the poet quickly recalled the phrase written by Saint Paul in 1 Corinthians 15:18, "fallen asleep in Christ".

Putting the two phrases together she began mulling over the words "Asleep in Jesus". "The blessed dead who died in the Lord", she thought, "are not merely asleep but they are asleep in Jesus. The sleep of death which has taken hold of them is a gift of a loving and compassionate Heavenly Father, who 'gives his beloved sleep', only to give them a new awakening over on the other side." Thus it was, that, twelve years after her marriage at eighteen to Major William MacKay of the 68th Light Infantry, Margaret MacKay sat down and wrote her funeral hymn, "Asleep in Jesus", which contained these lines:

Asleep in Jesus! blessed sleep, From which none ever wakes to weep!
A calm and undisturbed repose, Unbroken by the last of foes.
Asleep in Jesus! peaceful rest, Whose waking is supremely blest!
No fear, no woe, shall dim that hour That manifests the Saviour's power.

Her four stanzas were first published the year they were written, in "The Amethyst", and were included in a later publication of the poet herself in the 1854 edition of her book "Thoughts Redeemed".

Her own husband, a distinguished officer who became a Lieutenant Colonel, "fell upon eternal sleep" in 1845, the year they were to have celebrated the silver anniversary of their wedding, and Margaret MacKay outlived him for forty-two years before passing away at Cheltenham, on January 5, 1887, in the spirit and radiance of the final stanza of her most famous hymn:

Asleep in Jesus! O for me, May such a blissful refuge be!
Securely shall my ashes lie, Waiting the summons from on high.

In thus writing her finest poem on the subject of Heaven, Mrs. Margaret MacKay joins the host of women who, like her, have voiced their feelings and convictions about eternal life in poems and hymns that have outlived their own day and whose usefulness has extended far beyond the narrow confines of their own generations: Mrs. Anne Ross Cousin, author of "The sands of time are sinking" popularly known as "Immanuel's Land"; Fanny Crosby, who wrote "Safe in the arms of Jesus"; Mrs. Jessie Brown Pounds who gave us "Beautiful Isle of Somewhere"; Sarah Doudney, who penned "The Christian's Goodnight", and Phoebe Cary, whose poem "One sweetly solemn thought" is a perennial favorite throughout Christendom.

2.

BEAUTIFUL ISLE OF SOMEWHERE

The Ministerial Association of Portsmouth, Virginia annually sponsors a week of Inspirational Services, and the various participating denominations in the Association take turns in inviting their leading preachers to speak during the designated week. In 1957 the Christian Churches of the city were charged with the responsibility of providing an outstanding minister of their denomination as the visiting preacher for the series of services. The Association, instead of voting to begin the week with the traditional Sunday afternoon gathering, accepted the motion of this writer to begin with a great united Hymn Festival in which all of the Churches connected with the Association would participate. When I was asked to plan and direct this first city-wide hymn sing, I chose as the topic for the Festival "Hymns of all Churches", and explained that it was my desire to show those who assembled for an hour of worship through singing that we are indebted to every denominational group for the hymns we sing and love.

For example, Baptist clergymen wrote "He leadeth me" and "America", while Presbyterians gave us "This is my father's world" and "O love that wilt not let me go". Episcopalian ministers wrote "Abide with me" and "Holy, holy, holy", a Lutheran "A mighty fortress is our God", a Congregationalist "My faith looks up to Thee", a Jew "The Lord is my shepherd", Roman

Catholics "Jesus the very thought of thee" and "Shepherd of tender youth" while a Unitarian provided "Nearer my God to thee", a Quaker "Dear Lord and father of mankind" and a Salvation Army worker "The old rugged cross."

A little while before the 8 p.m. hour when the evening service was scheduled to begin, I met the distinguished clergyman from Indianapolis, a representative of the Christian Church, who was to speak briefly during the Hymn Festival and preach each morning and night during the following five days. He asked me what I had planned for the evening, and I outlined the type of program I intended to follow.

And, when it suddenly occurred to me that I had not selected a single hymn from the pen of a leading hymn writer of his denomination, I swallowed my pride, confessed to him my ignorant blunder, and asked, "Who is the outstanding hymn writer of your Church?" When he seemed as non-plussed as I had been a few moments earlier, I breathed more easily.

After a brief pause, he turned and said, "To tell you the truth, I really don't know."

I smiled and said to myself, "If he, one of the prominent clergymen of his Church, doesn't know, then no one can accuse me of ignoring his denomination in the selection of hymns for tonight's program."

Just before we went into the Sanctuary of the Church in which the meetings were to be held, the visiting pastor took my arm and said, "I believe that the wife of one of our preachers wrote several gospel songs, and I think her name was Pounds, or something like that." I nodded in appreciation, and immediately, in my mind's eye, saw the name "Jessie Brown Pounds" at the left hand side of a gospel song entitled "The way of the cross leads home."

"I know of her", I said. "She wrote 'The way of the cross leads home', didn't she?"

"Yes," he replied. "She was the wife of one of our leading ministers in Indianapolis."

So, that night, expressing my regrets at being unable to unearth a great hymn from the pen of a minister or laymen connected with The Christian Church (and to this day I become confused when trying to differentiate between that branch of the Church that united with the Congregationalists to form The Congregational-

15

Christian Church, and those who are more familiarly known as Christian Disciples) I referred to Mrs. Pounds and her gospel song by name and determined to learn more about her before conducting a similar program anywhere else in the future.

It was some time later that I discovered that Jessie Brown had been born in Hiram, Ohio, August 31, 1861, the year the Civil War began, and had quite early given evidence of unusual literary skill. In fact, by the time she was a teen-ager, she was writing regularly for several newspapers and religious periodicals. When music-publisher J. H. Fillmore came across some of her work he was impressed enough to suggest that they collaborate on several songs, which they did with varying degrees of success. Later she worked with Fillmore's younger brother, Charles, in similar undertakings. Prior to her marriage, she was offered a responsible editorial position with the Standard Publishing Company of Cincinnati, performing her duties in an outstanding manner until 1896, when she became the wife of Reverend John E. Pounds, who was serving as pastor of the Central Christian Church of Indianapolis at the time.

One Sunday morning shortly after her marriage, the young bride did not feel well enough to attend the services in her husband's Church, so she remained at home while he left to assume the usual Sunday morning responsibilities of a busy city preacher. While she had always hesitated to try her hand at writing poems or hymns about heaven, since she considered the theme beyond the limitations of her talent, this particular morning she began to study the subject in a different light. The kind of poems that painted heaven in exaggerated terms of "lives of ease and grandeur" seemed selfish to her, while others were so "sickly sentimental" as to be unworthy of the majesty of their theme. To Mrs. Pounds, her faith in heaven was "grounded upon her faith in the existence of God, and in His goodness", and such a faith "cannot be in vain". Soon she was not concerning herself so much with where heaven is, or what heaven is, as she was with the fact that "we leave the present to God's love and care" and "heaven will thereby almost take care of itself."

When her husband returned from the morning service, she said to him, "My hymn is written". Handing him a sheet of paper, he read aloud the title "Beautiful Isle Of Somewhere".

16

The first of her three stanzas and the chorus, contained these words:

Somewhere the sun is shining, Somewhere the songbirds dwell;
Hush then thy sad repining, God lives, and all is well.
Somewhere, somewhere, beautiful isle of somewhere;
Land of the true, where we live anew, Beautiful isle of somewhere.

Composer John Sylvester Fearis (1867-1932) set music to Mrs. Pounds' stanzas and the hymn was copyrighted and published the very next year, in 1897. Fearis, born in Richland, Iowa, moved to Chicago where he made quite a name for himself as a composer and publisher, turning out hundreds of anthems, operettas and gospel songs. In fact, one little ditty he dashed off for a group of girls on a camping trip, a song he called "Little Sir Echo", was remembered by one of the campers, who, when she grew up, recorded the song and made it one of the popular hits of the thirties.

For thirteen years prior to his death at Lake Geneva, Wisconsin, September 2, 1932, Fearis served as choir master of a large Lutheran Church in Chicago.

From the pen of Jessie Brown Pounds came other popular gospel songs, among them "The way of the cross leads home" which Charles Gabriel set to music and copyrighted in 1906; "The touch of his hand on mine", with the music composed by Henry P. Morton and copyrighted in 1913; "I want to live closer to Jesus" on which she collaborated with Mrs. C. M. Alexander. "Tell the promises over to me," another favorite with music by Mr. Benke, was more popular during the first quarter of this century than it has been since. Other Fearis tunes are still included in collections of gospel songs, the next in favor to "Beautiful Isle" being his music for Lizzie DeArmond's poem "In the cleft of the rock", dated 1901.

Prior to her death in 1921 at the age of sixty, the wife of the Christian clergyman had the joy of knowing that her sentimental song about heaven had been accepted by her fellow-Christians in the spirit in which she had penned her stanzas, and was being used of God to comfort many believers in their hours of sorrow.

3.

BEYOND THE SUNSET

Gospel song-writer Frank C. Huston had the joy of living to see one of his compositions, "It Pays to Serve Jesus," accepted by the Church, but, undoubtedly, it was an even greater source of joy to him that he had the privilege of encouraging a young couple to follow in his footsteps and write, sing, and publish their own original gospel hymns, songs and choruses.

When "The Singing Brocks" had become widely-known as authors, composers and song-leaders, Mr. Brock confessed, "We would not have kept on writing songs if it had not been for the encouragement and help of Frank C. Huston".

Virgil P. Brock, an active religious worker who had served his Lord in many varied capacities from Church janitor to Sunday School teacher and song-leader was ordained as a minister of the Christian Church when a youth of nineteen. It was during his pastorate at the Christian Church in Greens Fork, Indiana that he met the girl he was to marry, Blanche Marie Kerr.

Blanche, the daughter of Dr. and Mrs. James D. Kerr, a local physician and his wife, had been born in Greens Fork, Indiana, February 3, 1888 and had received her early education in the public schools of her native town. Later she had studied voice and piano at the Conservatory of Music in Indianapolis and at the American Conservatory in Chicago. When Virgil Brock met her, Blanche was serving as piano accompanist as well as soloist for a traveling evangelist. This type of religious work was not new to the accomplished musician, for she had played the piano for a three-week series of special services when she was only twelve years old.

In addition to serving God with her developing musical talents, Blanch Kerr, like her husband-to-be, had taught Sunday School and directed a Church orchestra and choir. Their mutual interest in musical activities naturally drew them together, and it was not long before their expected engagement was announced.

On September 24, 1914, Virgil Brock and Blanche Kerr became husband and wife and for the next few years they travelled together, handling the musical side of many revival and evangelistic services.

In addition to directing the music, Virgil handled advance publicity, led in the erection of several tabernacles, and supervised many other matters involved in a successful evangelistic campaign. Their first gospel song was inspired by a conversation with a travelling salesman who belonged to the Gideons, the group of devoted Christian salesmen who place Bibles in hotels and other public places and carry on other activities of this nature.

When this particular "Gideon" arose to speak at one of the meetings in which the Brocks were assisting, he said several times, "He's a wonderful Saviour to me." This phrase made such a deep impression upon Virgil that he went to sleep brooding about it, only to waken suddenly at four o'clock the next morning singing the Chorus,

"For he's a wonderful Saviour to me, He's a wonderful Saviour to me.
I was lost in sin but Jesus took me in; He's a wonderful Saviour to me."

Naturally Mrs. Brock awoke a bit surprised at what was going on, and Virgil soon persuaded her to get up and pick out his melody on the piano, a request with which she complied so she could get back to bed and finish her sleep before sunrise.

The following day, they worked out the four stanzas. "He's A Wonderful Saviour To Me" was copyrighted by Homer Rodeheaver a year later, in 1918, and when it was published, Virgil P. Brock was listed as the author and Blanche Kerr Brock as the composer, although they both stated that all of their best hymns and gospel songs were the results of joint efforts and close collaboration.

From 1923 until 1936 the Brocks were engaged in evangelistic work for their denomination in and around Blanche's native state. The success that greeted their endeavours in Indianapolis and throughout Indiana encouraged them to enter the general evangelistic field in 1936, a decision which enabled them to work with larger and larger congregations farther and farther from home.

It was while they were the guests of Homer Rodeheaver at Winona Lake, Indiana in 1936 that the Brocks were inspired to write their most popular gospel hymn "Beyond the Sunset". Rainbow Point, the Rodeheaver home, is located on the eastern side of the lake, affording a remarkable view of the sunset across the water to the west.

This particular evening, as the Brocks and several other faculty members of the Rodeheaver School of Music were watching the beauty of the setting sun in the distance, a blind guest, Mr. Horace L. Burr, said, "I never saw a more beautiful sunset, and I have seen them around the world."

That a blind man should make such a startling statement stirred the soul of Virgil Brock, so he began to ask Burr the very obvious question that was on the lips or in the minds of all of the others.

"Horace," he began, "you always talk about seeing," whereupon the other man interrupted him and added, "I do see through the eyes of others. I see even beyond the sunset."

Virgil thought about the beautiful sunset and the even more beautiful phrase with which his blind friend had described it, and soon he was humming a melodious tune and forming words and phrases to match the simplicity of the music. His wife caught his enthusiasm, excused herself from the supper table for a few minutes, went to the piano nearby and began picking out the melody he had begun singing.

Soon the entire first stanza was completed with almost effortless ease, and, almost before her host and hostess missed her, she returned to her place at the table and resumed her meal where she had left off just a few short moments earlier.

Virgil polished off his phrases and lines to conform to the meter of Blanche's interpretation of the music, and soon finished the first stanza:

"Beyond the sunset, O blissful morning, When with our Saviour heav'n is begun.
Earth's toiling ended, O glorious dawning; Beyond the sunset, when day is done."

A threatening storm later that night led him to write the second stanza in which he included the line "No storms will threaten, no fears annoy." Then, as he remembered how Grace Pierce Burr had guided her husband during the years of his blindness by the touch of her outstretched hand, he wrote in the third stanza that "Beyond the sunset a hand will guide me," while the fourth and final stanza spoke of the "glad reunion with our dear loved ones who've gone before."

When the Rodeheaver Company published "Beyond the Sunset" and copyrighted it that same year, 1936, Virgil was listed as the author and Blanche as the composer, while the song was "Dedicated to Horace L. and Grace Pierce Burr," a loving tribute to the couple who had inspired it.

In a letter from Frank C. Huston dated November 5, 1958, the man whose words of encouragement had started the Brocks on the road to musical success wrote, "The Brocks sang at both my Father's and Mother's funeral, and it has been our understanding that they should conduct my funeral when it occurred, as I am about ten years older than they, but now they can't be there, both of them, as Blanche went home first of the company."

Blanche, a member of ASCAP, who lived to see her name included in "Who's Who Of American Women," went to her heavenly home from Winona Lake, Indiana, on Friday, January 3, 1958. Virgil and their only son, James W. Brock, Ph.D., of Northwestern University, survived.

Huston continued, "It was not my lot to preach Blanche's funeral, as I was unable to make the trip, (Huston was eighty-six years old at the time) so Virgil had me make a recording, which I did here, which was given at her funeral."

It was through Frank Huston's thoughtfulness that I received much of this information, one of his letters containing this tribute to the Brocks. "I should feel that I was not their friend should I fail to let you know them as I have known them for these many years."

Left behind, husband Virgil and long-time friend Frank look "beyond the sunset" to the "glad reunion" of which the Brocks had sung in the closing stanza of their finest gospel song:

> "In that fair homeland we'll know no parting,
> Beyond the sunset, forevermore."

4.

DOES JESUS CARE?

Every sincere Christian feels that the words of the Negro spiritual, "Sometimes I'm up, Sometimes I'm down, Sometimes I'm almost to the ground", are descriptive of his own Christian experience, for few are the believers who have not, in their own spiritual lives, run the gamut from hopeful optimism to despairing pessimism, to say nothing of the days when one cannot tell whether he is up, down, or just somewhere in the "misty flats" in between the two. Like St. Peter of old, we find ourselves confessing Christ as "the Son of the living God" one moment, only to have Jesus say to us "Get thee behind me, Satan," the very next moment, as we attempt to persuade him not to go to Jerusalem to face certain death at the hands of his enemies.

So it is not surprising to know that the Rev. Frank Graeff (1860-1919) an honored minister of the Philadelphia Conference of the Methodist Church, was referred to as a "spiritual optimist" possessing a "holy magnetism" as well as a "childlike faith", although he, too, knew moments to deep despair, when, like the Big Fisherman, he felt himself sinking beneath the waves on stormy Galilee, and reached out his hand, calling on the Lord to save him, lest he perish. Since only those people are capable of great faith who have known tremendous doubt, and find spiritual certainty only after having passed through the dark valley of sincere questioning, Graeff's experience is not difficult to understand.

Born in the coal mining town of Tamaqua, Pennsylvania, December 19, 1860, and reared in this well-known Pennsylvania German country, he early felt the call to the Christian ministry, and, after having completed his education, applied for membership in the Philadelphia Conference of the Methodist Church. His "days of preparation" having stood him in good stead, he was admitted to the Conference in 1890, his thirtieth year. Four years later on March 1, 1894, he was married to Miss Mary Lourene Mauger, the daughter of a brother minister in the same Conference, and entered upon a ministry that was to see him serving ten appointments in his Conference over a span of nearly thirty years.

His methodical habits as preacher and pastor were early appreciated by his brethren in the ministry, and it came as no surprise to them when he was asked to serve his Conference as assistant statistical secretary, and later as statistical secretary, posts he was to occupy with distinction for nearly a quarter of a century. Only those who are statistically minded can fully appreciate the responsibilities connected with and the intricate details involved in filling such a position in the Church, especially when the recipient serves unselfishly in that capacity for twenty-five years. But Graeff proved himself more than a student of numbers, for he began turning his talents in other directions, and soon was gaining for himself an enviable reputation as an author of children's stories. Those who knew and loved him best spoke tenderly about his devotion to the little children in his several parishes, a characteristic all the more remarkable in view of the fact that he and his wife never had any children. But the love he would have lavished on his own, he gave in full measure to those whom God had committed to his care as pastor, preacher, shepherd and friend. When he followed the playful antics of his wife's twin sisters as they grew up, he became so intrigued with their childhood experiences that he made them the subject of the only full-length book he was ever to write, a volume entitled "The Minister's Twins".

A brother minister says of these years of Graeff's active ministry, "He was a gracious personality, greatly beloved by the people in his churches. He was a solicitous pastor, with his heart aglow for his people and sympathetic to their needs." As such a watchful shepherd, he served these appointments in his Conference: Bangor Circuit; Somerton; Wesley; Bethany, Emanuel and Summerfield, Philadelphia; Toyersford; Haws Avenue, Norristown; Fairhill, Philadelphia and Cheltenham. Claflin University honored him with the degree of Doctor of Divinity in 1911.

His nephew and namesake, Rev. Frank Graeff Mauger, who also became a minister in the same Methodist Conference, spoke lovingly of his favorite uncle's sense of humor as well as his gracious generosity, illustrating the first by telling of the time Graff took one of his wife's pies as a gift to a neighbor, only to discover later that the crusts of that particular batch were unusually tough. Undaunted, the fun-loving preacher took a hatchet to the neighbour with the explanation that it was to be used in cutting the pie! When his nephew was about to leave home for school, his uncle met him at Wanamaker's Store in Philadelphia and bought him a suit of clothes, bidding him goodbye with this simple but unforgettable admonition, "Frank, be good!"

Although he was widely popular as "The Sunshine Minister", George Sanville suggests that at one time in his life Frank Graeff became very despondent, questioning the truths he had previously preached with such certainity, and doubting the goodness of the God whom he had convincingly and constantly extolled as a loving heavenly Father. Possibly the burdens of his people weighed heavily upon his heart, a weight that many pastors find grevious to be borne. Or it may have been at a time when he was so physically worn that his spiritual life mirrored the exhaustion of his body. Nevertheless, it was during those long, trying days that Frank Graeff sought for solace, strength and rest in the pages of the Holy Scriptures, feeding his barren soul upon Him who is the living bread, and quenching his spiritual thirst with Him who is the water of life. The one verse that comforted him during those days of depression contained but four words, three of them being words of one syllable, "He careth for you."

Out of that period of night, the minister emerged slowly into the radiant light of another dawn and soon was recounting his experience in a question and answer hymn, written in somewhat the same style as "Art thou weary, Art thou languid, Art thou sore distressed?" which asks a question and then answers it with a bold affirmation of the Christian faith. Graeff, however, did not state his question and answer in the same stanza, but made of every stanza a four-line question, and of the Chorus, a four-line affirmative reply. This is what he asked, in part:

Does Jesus care when my heart is pained Too deeply for mirth or song;
As the burdens press, and the cares distress, And the way grows weary and long?

While this was his reply to his own question:

Oh, yes, He cares; I know He cares; His heart is touched with
   my grief;
When the days are weary, the long nights dreary, I know my
   Saviour cares.

It remained only for Mr. J. Lincoln Hall (1866-1930) to
compose his music and the Methodist pastor's poem began to
wing its way into the hearts of Christian people the world over.
Mr. Hall later told this writer's father, Rev. S. K. Emurian, at
the time Hall was assisting him in editing Emurian's musical setting of "The Lord's Prayer" for publication, that he considered
his tune for Graeff's poem the most inspired piece of music he
was ever privileged to compose. It is because so many other
Christians have gone through similar nights of doubt and despair,
that Graeff's gospel song touches so many hearts so deeply.

The gifted clergyman lived only fifty-nine years, passing away
on July 29, 1919, at Ocean Grove, New Jersey, being buried in
the Riverside Cemetery, Norristown, Pennsylvania several days
later, following funeral services at the St. James Church, Olney,
Philadelphia. The loved ones whom he left behind could find
comfort in reading the question he posed in the final stanza of
his gospel hymn:

"Does Jesus care when I've said 'good-by' To the dearest on
earth to me?"

For he had replied with this word of assurance, wrought out on
the anvil of his own heart, "Oh, Yes, He cares, I know He cares!"

5.

EVEN ME

Mrs. Elizabeth Codner opened the Bible to Psalm 72:6, and read aloud "He shall come down like rain upon the mown grass; as showers that water the earth," and then said to herself, "God works his miracles of grace in strange and unexpected ways. Sometimes he appears in an earthquake, and sometimes in a pillar of fire; at other times he is present in a clap of thunder or a flash of lightning and then again we know He is near when we hear His still, small voice. He stops some sinners suddenly as he appeared to St. Paul in a blinding flash of light on the Damascus Road, and to Moses, centuries earlier, in a burning bush on the rocky slope of Mount Sinai. Yet there are sincere and devout believers to whom he has come as a soft and gentle rain, quenching their thirst after righteousness, and satisfying them, fulfilling the promise He gave in the beautitude 'Blessed are they that hunger and thirst after righteousness, for they shall be filled'."

Looking again through the Old Testament, she came across this verse in Ezekiel 34:29, in the ancient seer's prophecy about the New Kingdom God was to establish after the trials and tribulations of the exile were passed, "And I will make them and the places round about my hill a blessing; and I will cause the shower to come down in his season; there shall be showers of blessing." She paused as she thought once more of the dry and arid regions of Palestine, the wells that were dug and filled in by enemies only to be re-opened again years later, the cisterns that captured the life-giving water when rain fell from the skies and the conduits that brought the precious fluid from distant springs into the pools in Jerusalem and other cities where large groups of people demanded more and more water for all of their many and varied needs. She experienced afresh the impact of the Lord's words, when he said he was not only the bread of life but also the water of life and thought she knew how the Samaritan woman must have felt when, weary with carrying water to and from Jacob's well for so many years, she heard Jesus speak to her of "living water" and thought, for a moment, that all her days of pitcher-bearing drudgery were over.

The expression from Ezekiel, "showers of blessing", fastened itself upon her mind, and refused to let go, plaguing her to such an extent that she felt she would be glad to be rid of it once and for all. When the occasion finally presented itself, it was not in the least what she expected. For a group of young people came to visit Rev. and Mrs. Codner in their home in Islington, London, England, one afternoon in 1860, Elizabeth's thirty-sixth year, bearing exciting tidings of a great spiritual awakening which was sweeping over certain cities and counties of Ireland. Some of the more sensitive youngsters had been so deeply impressed with the services they had attended on the Emerald Isle that the magic spell which had been cast upon them by the fervent preaching of some of Christendom's outstanding preachers seemingly could not be broken. All they could talk about in public or speak of in private conversation was the impact of the religious revival on their own lives and the miracles of grace they saw God work in the lives of many others.

And, listening intently to their vivid descriptions and dramatic portrayals of the meetings in which they had participated, Mrs. Codner thought to herself, "They must not be satisfied to let their own fleece remain dry. I must press upon them the privilege and responsibility of getting an individual share in the out-poured blessing." Then, with startling suddenness, the words of Ezekiel flashed into her mind, and she said, "While the Lord is pouring ᴑut such showers of blessing, pray some drops will fall on each one of you."

The following Sunday morning, early in 1860, Mrs. Codner did not feel well enough to attend the public services of worship in her husband's Church, so she remained at home. But she did not waste the hour in idle dreaming or while it away aimlessly and with no purpose in view. She spent that precious time thinking again of her young friends and of her admonition of the previous evening.

27

The more she thought of them and of her words of counsel and advice, the more she could see in her mind's eye the showers of blessing pouring down from heaven, while dry-souled sinners and thirsty saints reached out for some drops of the down-flowing flood. "O God," she found herself praying, "let some drops fall, not only on those young people, but on me, and on everyone who is thirsty of heart." In a few moments, she found herself creating words and phrases, lines and stanzas, and, almost before she knew it, she was writing down a hymn containing those words:

Lord, I hear of showers of blessing, Thou art scattering full and free;
Showers, the thirsty land refreshing; Let some drops now fall on me.
Even me.

In subsequent stanzas, she addressed her Master in pleading tones, saying, "Pass me not, O gracious Father", and "Pass me not, O tender Saviour" (This was eight years before the American poet Fanny Crosby (1820-1915) was to write her hymn "Pass me not, O gentle Saviour"), and "Pass me not, O Mighty Spirit". In those stanzas she begged the Lord to pour out his mercy upon her, to call her, to speak his word of power to her and to magnify all of his great goodness in her own life.

With no thought whatsoever of sending her seven simple stanzas beyond the circle of her own friends and acquaintances, she had copies printed and distributed, and it came as a shocking surprise to her when requests began to come from far and near for more and more copies of "Even Me". In her own words "The Lord took it quite out of my own hands" and used it for his own glory, and soon it was being read from hundreds of pulpits and circulated among Christian people by the tens of thousands.

When American composer William B. Bradbury (1816-1868) discovered the stanzas he quickly set them to music repeating the last line and the two key words as a Chorus or Refrain, and "Even me" began to be sung as well as read in numerous Churches throughout Christendom. The author later wrote, "The point of the hymn, in its close and individual application, is in the 'Even me' at the end of the verse."

As for the use of her stanzas, she granted her permission gladly and readily to every request, saying, "I thankfully commit them

28

to whoever desires to use them in the services of our blessed Master."

Mrs. Codner published several small volumes, among them "The Missionary Ship" and "The Bible in the Kitchen", and was associated for some years with the work of the Mildmay Protestant Mission in London. Seven years after she wrote her most famous hymn, she prepared a companion poem, "Lord, to thee my heart ascending", dated 1867, but it never received the response which greeted "Even me".

Doubtless her husband was grieved when his wife could not attend Church services that providential Sunday morning in 1860, but it must have gladdened his heart when he learned later that the poem Elizabeth Codner (1824-1919) wrote while he was preaching, was being used of God in such a marvelous way.

The poet's prayer, uttered in the closing stanza of her hymn, which she included in its entirety in her book "Among the Brambles and other Lessons from Life" was answered far beyond her fondest dreams, for she had said:

Pass me not, thy lost one bringing, Bind my heart, O Lord, to thee;
While the streams of life are springing, Blessing others, O Bless me.
Even me.

6.

FACE TO FACE

The death of Rev. Grant Colfax Tullar was important enough to be mentioned in the stately columns of the erudite daily newspaper, The New York Times, indicating something of the importance the editors of that scholarly journal attached to the knowledge of his passing.

Under the dateline of May 20, 1950, and captioned "Special to the New York Times" this notice from Ocean Grove, New

Jersey, appeared, "The Rev. Grant C. Tullar, composer and publisher of religious music, died in the Methodist Home for the Aged here this morning. His age was 80. Mr. Tullar, who was noted as a Methodist evangelist, formerly was a member of the music publishing firm of Meredith and Tullar, New York, specializing in church music. He was a composer of numerous hymns, among them the widely known 'Face To Face.' He was a graduate of Hackettstown Theological Seminary, and made his home in East Orange for several years before coming here to live in the Methodist Home. Surviving are his widow, a son, H. W. Tullar of Lancaster, Pennsylvania, and a daughter, Mrs. L. A. Pratt, of Redlands, California."

Of the many hymnals and gospel song books Tullar edited, with the capable assistance of other musicians, singers, composers and associate editors, and of the many original stanzas and tunes he wrote or composed, only "Face to Face" merited mention in this brief obituary notice, convincing proof that of all his numerous compositions, this alone gained the universal approval of Christendom which assured it a measure of immortality. But, strangely enough, when pastor Tullar composed his famous tune which is now inextricably linked with the stanzas of Mrs. Frank A. Breck, her words were as far from his mind as "the east is from the west". His personal account of the unusual incidents which led up to the production of this gospel hymn give them the note of authority and authenticity which a composer alone can supply, since the passing of years has given rise to numerous anecdotes and fanciful narratives which are too far removed from the truth to even deny, but which, nevertheless, continue to spread by word of mouth, until truth and fiction are blended in an assortment of fact and fancy that defies analysis.

The composer himself dates the music 1898, while the additional fact that "Face to Face" was copyrighted in 1899, bears witness to the truthfulness of his statement. It was during the preacher-composer's stay in a Methodist parsonage in Rutherford, New Jersey, just before the turn of the century, that the events leading up to the composing of his tune took place. During a series of evangelistic services in the local Methodist Church, Tullar was a guest of the pastor and his wife. One particular afternoon, the three of them had spent several busy hours calling upon the sick members of the congregation, arriving at the parsonage with just enough time before the evening service to wash up, grab a bite of supper and hurry over to the Church. When they finally managed to sit around the kitchen table for a hasty supper, everything seemed to be in order save for the fact that the hostess, in the rush of the previous few minutes, had overlooked replenishing the jelly dish. Knowing their guest's fondness for jelly, the host pastor and his wife refused to help themselves to the tiny dab that remained in the dish from the last meal, insisting that their guest enjoy what little there was left. Undaunted, he proceeded to do just that, smiling as he picked it up with his knife and said, "So this is all for me, is it?"

In an instant, his fertile brain was hard at work, for the three-word phrase "all for me", seemed to be almost too good to be true. "It's a perfect theme for a new gospel song," Tullar said to himself, and in a few minutes, he was seated at the piano in the parsonage living room, picking out a tune and thinking up some original lines for the music simultaneously. In an unbelievably short while, he was singing, to the amazement of the local pastor and his wife, an entirely new gospel song to a brand new gospel tune, "All for me the Saviour suffered, All for me he bled and died." His host was so enthusiastic that he begged Tullar to let him sing it at the evening service, but the author-composer felt it needed a little polishing up before being sprung on the public, and promised to do so only after putting the finishing touches on some of the lines the next morning.

However, the following morning fate intervened, and "All for me the Saviour suffered" never get beyond the manuscript stage. For the postman brought Mr. Tullar a letter from Mrs. Frank A. Breck, in which she enclosed several of her original poems for his consideration, Tullar already having set several of her poems to music. Mrs. Breck (1855-1934), a Vermont native who spent several years in New Jersey before moving out west to make her home in Portland, Oregon, was, in the words of one of her five daughters, "a deeply religious life-long Presbyterian" who, although knowing nothing about music, "had a keen sense of rhythm" that enabled her to write stanzas for many popular gospel hymns and songs. Most of her poems were written during the time she rested from her numerous household chores by rocking one of her little ones in a favorite kitchen chair, a baby on one arm, and a notebook on the other.

Quickly looking through the new batch of poems, Mr. Tullar spotted one that immediately commanded his attention. He read half-aloud the words on the paper before him, inspired, he was convinced, by a phrase Paul had written in 1 Corinthians 13:12, "For now we see through a glass darkly, but then face to face". For Mrs. Breck had composed these lines for her publisher-composer:

"Face to face with Christ my Saviour, Face to face — what will it be,
When in rapture I behold Him, Jesus Christ who died for me?
Face to face shall I behold Him, Far beyond the starry sky;
Face to face, in all His glory, I shall see Him by and by."

Tullar could hardly believe his eyes and ears as he suddenly realized that Mrs. Breck's stanzas fitted perfectly the tune he had composed the previous night for his own lines "All for me the Saviour suffered". Quickly singing his music to her lines, he realized that the new gospel hymn was a natural. The Christian public readily concurred, as "Face to Face" became the most popular of Tullar's tunes and Mrs. Breck's stanzas.

Other Breck successes included "Help somebody today" and "When love shines in", neither one rivalling the perennial favorite, "Face to Face". Many other Tullar stanzas and tunes are to be found in THE BIBLE SCHOOL HYMNAL, one of the many Tullar-Meredith publications, as well as in THE VOICE OF PRAISE, a 1904 Hall-Mack Company song book, among them being "He did not die in vain", a Breck-Tullar production.

But in the years that have passed since both the poet and composer met the Master face to face, this particular gospel hymn has maintained its popularity and seems destined to take its rightful place alongside many other splendid hymns of the same calibre that hold before Christian people the world over the assurance of the realization of Paul's prophetic words in the lives of each individual believer:

"Face to face, oh, blissful moment! Face to face — to see and know;
Face to face with my Redeemer, Jesus Christ, who loves me so."

7

GOD'S BEST FOR ME

The year 1907 was a memorable one in the life of the Armenian immigrant, Sisag Krikor Emurian, who, having graduated from Anatolia College, the American Congregational Missionary College in Marsovan, Asia Minor, with a Bachelor of Arts degree at the age of 19 in 1893, had made his successful and dramatic escape from Turkey to the safety and security of the United States five years later in 1898. The son of a pioneer Protestant clergyman in the province of Cappadocia, Asia Minor, Rev. Krikor B. Emurian, "S.K." remained at his Alma Mater for four years following his graduation, serving as the first music teacher on the faculty of that distinguished institution. During those years he played the college organ, directed the choir and glee club, and composed many sacred and secular songs which soon became the folksongs of his people. His honored father had been won to the Protestant faith while working in a hospital in Constantinople during the Crimean War, and it was while serving in this capacity that he met Florence Nightingale during one of her hospital tours that radically revolutionized the profession of nursing.

When the Turks embarked upon another of their systematic and cruel massacres of the Armenian people in 1896, the young music professor was thrown into a dirty dungeon along with other faculty members and students who were attending the American college in their quest for a Christian education. Upon his release, his parents and friends urged him to attempt to escape to America, the land of freedom from which his teachers and missionary professors had come. When the American flag saved the lives of the student body by holding back a blood-thirsty mob of mountain Turks known as Kurds, Sisag decided that it was America for him. Bidding farewell to the familiar sights of the village of Moonjison, sixteen miles from Caesarea, where he had been born on May 3, 1874, and kissing his father, mother, brothers and sisters goodbye for the last time, he set his sights on the western horizon.

After many thrilling adventures, narrow escapes and unbelievable struggles, he landed in New York City in September 1898, with only five dollars in his pocket. Borrowing money from a famous Armenian missionary-educator, Rev. Harutune Jenanyan, of Philadelphia, whose eldest daughter, Grace, he was to marry ten years later, Sisag pressed on to Oberlin College in Ohio, where he wanted to perfect his musical training to further his aspiration to sing Grand Opera. Blessed with a remarkable baritone voice, and well grounded in the rudiments of instrumental and vocal music, he could have made quite a name for himself on the stage, but God had other plans for him which were revealed in conversations with Oberlin's president, Dr. Henry Churchill King, and one of her most prominent Seminary professors, Edward Increase Bosworth. Under their guidance and encouragement, "S.K." entered the Theological Seminary to prepare himself for the Christian ministry, to which his own father had already dedicated the greater part of his life.

In 1901, after three years of scrimping, saving, studying and serving, the talented Armenian received his Bachelor of Divinity degree and entered upon a twelve year period of unusual evangelistic endeavours that carried him into many states of the expanding union and into the pulpits of some of the leading Protestant Churches of the north and north-west. Following a successful evangelistic tour of several Ohio Churches, Emurian was invited to preach in the Baptist Churches of Medina, and Fairport, New York in March, 1906. That visit proved a providential one in two respects, for it was at Fairport that he met Mr. Henry Addison DeLand, who founded the city of DeLand, Florida, and DeLand University, soon renamed for his "noble friend John B. Stetson" and now known as Stetson University.

The great philanthropist befriended the "foreign" preacher, and the friendship between the two men developed so deeply that "S.K." promised the older man he would name his first son for him, if ever God granted him the privilege of marrying and having a family of his own. That promise was fulfilled, for Emurian married Miss Grace Jenanyan in June, 1909, and their first son, born a year later, was named Henry, after Mr. DeLand.

The other fast friend the singing clergyman made during his visit to Medina, was a richly spiritual-souled physician, Dr. Emily F. Swett. It was at her invitation that Emurian joined a small party of friends in the summer of 1907, a few weeks after he became a full-fledged American citizen on April 1, 1907, and made his first trip to the historic religious conference ground at Northfield, Massachusetts, a place hallowed by the name and memory of the talented lay-preacher Dwight L. Moody. An interesting scrap book kept by his hostess during that memorable summer was presented to him in 1922, and is now cherished as a valued possession by the Emurian family. In it there is a photograph of "S.K." at the grave of the great Mr. Moody, a picture of peculiar interest for it was at the moment that he read the simple inscription on Moody's gravestone, "He that doeth the will of God abideth forever", that he resolved to set that passage of Scripture to music, an ambition realized a few years later when he composed one of his finest sacred solos based upon that phrase from St. John. But it was a poem with which one of the famous preachers closed a sermon one evening that especially caught the eye and ear of the thirty-three year old evangelist. The visitor stated that the poem came from the pen of Rev. A. B. Simpson, and was entitled "God's Best".

Emurian knew that Simpson had been a Presbyterian pastor in New York City before leaving that denomination to "carry on independent evangelistic work among the unchurched", a move that eventually resulted in the founding of the Christian Alliance for Home Missions and the International Missionary Alliance for Foreign Missions. The merging of those two bodies in 1897 created the Church now known familiarly as The Christian Missionary Alliance.

The first stanza of Simpson's poem burned itself into Emurian's heart for in it Simpson had said:

God has his best things for the few That dare to stand the test;
God has his second choice for those Who will not have his best.

To the composer-preacher, the poem was crying for a tune, and he felt that, providentially, it had been practically dropped into his lap. Some weeks later, he composed an appropriate tune, adding, in the custom of the day, a chorus all his own, which contained this prayer:

I want thy very best, I want thy very best.
O help me, Lord, refuse the rest, To get thy very best.

When he published a booklet containing several of his own gospel songs in 1913, "God's Best For Me" soon proved to be the most acceptable and rapidly became the most popular. After a pastorate of several years serving the Presbyterian Church in Fort Edward, New York, Emurian moved with his family to Norfolk, Virginia in 1918, becoming a minister of the Presbyterian Church in the United States (The Southern Presbyterian Church).

When Mr. R. E. Magill was asked to edit and compile a new songbook for that denomination, he secured the services of Mr. B. D. Ackley as Music Editor. Of all of Emurian's gospel songs, Ackley considered "God's Best For Me" the very best, and included it in "Premier Hymns" which the Presbyterians published in Richmond in 1926.

And he who wisely chose God's best for his own life, was providentially led from Armenia to Medina to Northfield to Virginia, where God richly blessed his ministry in a wide variety of ways, until at this writing in 1959, at the age of eighty-five, still actively preaching and singing his Master's praises, my father, Rev. S. K. Emurian, can sing with spiritual sincerity the closing stanza of his finest gospel song:

I want amid the victor throng, To hear my name confessed,
And hear my Saviour say at last, "Well done! you took the best."

8.

HAVE THINE OWN WAY

Among the many self-styled Messiahs who have appeared on the American scene during the past century, none was more colorful or dramatic than the man who called himself "Elijah III", a congregational minister named John Alexander Dowie, whose parish ranged from the rocky coasts of Scotland to the primitive bush country of Australia. When he made his triumphal entry into the United States in 1888, he explained to curious questioners that Elijah I was naturally the Old Testament prophet of Mt. Carmel fame, while Elijah II was none other than John the Baptist, the fore-runner of Jesus, of New Testament lineage; while he, having felt the mantle of greatness and glory falling upon his not unwilling shoulders, regarded himself as the second re-incarnation of the fiery prophet from whom he took his title.

Advertising himself as a specialist in the art of divine healing (direct healing, that is, in contrast to the indirect healing performed by physicians and doctors who were trained in medical science), Dowie, a dynamic man possessing a magnetic personality, conducted a series of healing missions in Chicago during the last decade of the last century, finally climaxing his evangelistic campaign by organizing an entirely new religious denomination bearing the weighty and all-inclusive name of "The Christian Catholic Apostolic Church in Zion".

Among those who attended his healing sessions was Sarah Addison Pollard, a native of Bloomfield, Iowa, where she had been born on November 27, 1862. Although her first two names perpetuated the memories of her mother's sister Sarah and elder brother, Joseph Addison, this daughter of James and Rebecca Smith Pollard was nicknamed "Addie", a name which she bore with patience until her seventeenth year, when she herself adopted the name "Adelaide" perferring it to all the others, and it was as Adelaide A. Pollard that she was known from that moment on.

By the time she attended the first Dowie healing meetings in Chicago, she had completed her education at Denmark Academy in Iowa (1879-80), following that with further studies at Valparaiso, Indiana and a three-year course in elocution and physical culture at the Boston School of Oratory in Massachusetts.

When she finished her training in New England, she returned to Chicago, making her home with her Mother in The Windy City, earning her livelihood by teaching in several private schools there in addition to publishing an original phonic method of instructing students in reading.

For some years Adelaide had suffered from diabetes, and one day in Chicago, following a period of rapidly declining health, she collapsed in a diabetic coma, whereupon a friend, Miss Lily L. Waller, took her to a Dowie meeting, where she was treated by Elijah III in person. The immediate result of this dramatic experience was that Miss Pollard "rose up, testified and walked out of the service declaring herself completely and entirely healed".

That such was not the case became evident only too soon, and she continued to suffer from physical ailments and disabilities the rest of her life. However, her faith in Dowie and his ministry of healing was so strong that for a time she associated herself with him, assisting him in some of his healing sessions. As a part of her public ministry she began to hold religious services on the streets, even carrying a small portable organ with her so she could accompany the hymns she sang to the passersby.

It was but a brief step from the Dowie program to one of more intense emphasis upon Faith Healing, and soon she and Miss Waller, now her constant companion, took up with another travelling prophet, this time by the name of Sanford, who declared that the second coming of Christ was imminent, and who had, with a handful of deluded disciples, actually set up a Watch Tower, on the coast of Maine, which was manned by some of these devotees, who were to signal to the others the moment they saw the Lord appearing in clouds of glory enroute to call the ransomed of earth to the raptures of their heavenly homes!

During these years, Miss Pollard's staunchly Presbyterian family, friends and loved ones back in Iowa saw very little of her. She may have felt that they did not appreciate her personal craving for the dramatic and sensational in her religious life, but she notified them with her letters as to her whereabouts while they followed her with their prayers as long as she lived.

A nervous collapse in 1895 dispelled any doubts as to the permanent effects of a Dowie cure, and Adelaide was practically an invalid for more than a year. During that time she read Church history, and emerged with a determination to go to Africa as a missionary. Sanford tried in vain to raise the necessary funds up in Maine, but when he was unable to secure sufficient money with which to purchase a ship of his own, she abandoned the project and became associated with the Christian and Missionary Alliance Training School at Nyack, New York, teaching there for several years. It was during the ups and downs of this time in her life that Adelaide Pollard, taking her inspiration from a close study of the Holy Scriptures, penned her autobiographical hymn, the only one by which her memory is perpetuated, "Have thine own way, Lord", the first stanza of which was based upon the figures of speech found in Jeremiah 18:1-6:

> "Have thine own way, Lord, Have thine own way;
> Thou art the Potter, I am the clay;
> Mould me and make me After thy will,
> While I am waiting, yielded and still."

Her second stanza revealed her familiarity with the Bible, for she based it on the phrase "whiter than snow", found in Psalm 51:7, while her third stanza, which spoke of God's all-sufficient power, was, no doubt, inspired by the words of Jesus, "All power is given unto me in heaven and eatrh", Matthew 28:18, while the fourth and final stanza, which was a prayer that Christ would so fill her with His spirit so that others would see "Christ only, always, living in me" was taken from the affirmation of Paul found in Galatians 2:20, "Christ liveth in me".

Although she penned this poem in 1902, her fortieth year, it was not until five years later that George Cole Stebbins (1846-1945) composed his beautiful tune, giving "Have thine own way" the wings of song that spread its message to the far corners of the Christian world.

The poet finally fulfilled her desire to become a missionary, sailing for Cape Town, South Africa sometime prior to the first World War. When the war broke out, she and her party were transferred to Scotland where they labored until the cessation of hostilities, whereupon she returned to New York and resumed her ministry in the New England states.

Illness and suffering plagued her declining years, while disappointments also must have added to her weight of woe. To this day some people recall how John Alexander Dowie and a trainload of his followers invaded New York City, hoping to capture that metropolis with a series of services in Madison Square Garden, only to discover that the city's reputation as "the graveyard of evangelists" was only too true.

Miss Pollard must have shared Dowie's heart-ache at this unexpected tragedy, since she regarded him as her spiritual mentor, father and advisor.

In 1901 Dowie founded the community of Zion, Illinois as a theocracy with Elijah III as its first "Apostle", a community that was headed by Wilbur Glen Voliva, a former Disciples of Christ minister, after Dowie's death. While Voliva made many headlines with his oft-repeated assertion that the earth was flat, he failed to develop into an object of veneration, but degenerated into a type of religious "screwball" who becomes merely an object of ridicule and pity.

As seventy-two year old Miss Adelaide was enroute from her New York City home to a New Jersey town during the Christmas Holidays in 1934 where she was to hold some religious meetings, she became critically ill in the New York City railroad station. She was rushed to a nearby Y. W. C. A. home where she died shortly thereafter, death being attributed to a ruptured appendix. She was buried beside her brother, Joesph Addison, in the cemetery at Fort Madison, Iowa, her finest hymn "Have thine own way", being read as she was reverently laid to rest.

Of her many hymns and poems, this sincere prayer alone survives, and if Sarah Addison Pollard had achieved only this claim to fame, her claim would have been justified for her hymn has become a favorite of believers of all ages, throughout the entire Christian world.

9.

HE KEEPS ME SINGING

The floods of sorrow and suffering that would have drowned many a lesser soul, released the song of hope and Christian joy in the burdened heart of Rev. Luther Burgess Bridgers (1884-1948). Born on February 14, 1884 in Margaretsville, North Carolina, Luther Bridgers spent most of his boyhood years in and around Norfolk and Portsmouth, Virginia. Many of the long-time residents of the cities recall that Luther and his family made their home on Bart Street, Portsmouth, for some time, during which the family was connected with the Owens Memorial Methodist

Church on Effingham Street. It was the congregation of this Methodist Church that formed the nucleus for the Elm Avenue Methodist Church of Portsmouth of which this writer is now pastor, after the church edifice which had housed the group on Effingham Street was sold to the Negroes who had taken possesion of most of the homes in the surrounding community. Some of the older members of the Elm Avenue Church remember hearing their parents speak of listening to Luther's father teach Sunday School in the old Owens Memorial building at the turn of the century.

However, after an all-too-brief stay in Tidewater, Virginia, the Bridgers family moved farther south and became adopted citizens of the state of Georgia. His devout mother had a profound influence upon little Luther's life, and it was the quality of her Christianity that inspired him to prepare for the Methodist ministry. In later years, after Luther's death, his widow paid her husband's mother this noble tribute, "She was a very devout Christian and explained many verses of Scripture to Luther when he was preparing for the ministry and all through his evangelistic life."

The year 1901 was a memorable one in the life of the adolescent itinerant preacher, because he began preaching full time then, although a stripling of seventeen, and he married Miss Sarah Veatch of Wilmore, Kentucky, whom he had met while studying at Asbury College in that city.

Early in his ministry, Luther Bridgers evidenced an unusual talent for handling large groups of worshippers, and became known far and wide as "a master of assemblies" with the power to sway great audiences with his spiritual appeal. Consequently, it came as no surprise to his family and friends that his ministry was blessed in a remarkable way in his local Church and that invitations to conduct special series of revival services came from leading Churches throughout Methodism.

During the first few years of his active ministry, God richly blessed Luther and his wife and three precious boys were born into their family. The future looked as bright as possible to the gifted young preacher when in 1910 he received and accepted an invitation to conduct a two-week series of evangelistic services not too far from the home of his wife's parents who lived at Harrodsburg, Kentucky. Leaving his family to the safe keeping of her

41

immediate relatives, Luther, now a maturing minister of twenty-six, kissed them goodbye, and hastened to reach his appointed destination in time for the opening service that very same night. Two glorious weeks later the services closed, all feeling the presence of the Holy Spirit in their hearts, and singing the praises of the pastor who had been so wonderfully used of God to convert the sinners and strengthen the saints in the local community.

Then, with a suddenness that cannot be explained or understood, at the very height of his ministerial success, with a promising future beckoning in the distance, tragedy struck the soul of Luther Bridgers. A long distance phone call in the dead of night appraised him of a disastrous fire that had completely consumed the house of his father-in-law, and taken the lives of his wife and three sons. A few days later, the ashes of the burned family were buried in the Bridgers burial plot in the cemetery at Wilmore, twenty miles from Harrodsburg.

The dark night that settled upon the soul of the young Methodist preacher can hardly be imagined by those who have never "loved long since and lost awhile". But the sustaining power of the Holy Spirit worked its miracle of grace in the distraught father's heart, and just as Paul and Silas had sung their inspired songs at midnight centuries before in the dark and dank dampness of a Philippian prison, so the Angel of God having touched the heart of Luther Bridgers, he began singing his "songs in the night", with such a fervor that the walls of the prison house of his sorrow fell to the ground, and he walked over them into the sunshine and freedom of the children of God. Then, with the memories of the past merging with the promises of the future, he wrote the words and music of a song that was his own spiritual autobiography, and which contained the secret of his spiritual triumph. To a tune that bore a resemblance to Englemann's popular piano solo "Melody Of Love", his first stanza contained these lines:

"There's within my heart a melody, Jesus whispers sweet and low,
Fear not, I am with thee, peace, be still, In all of life's ebb and
 flow."

The Chorus revealed his secret:

"Jesus, Jesus, Jesus, sweetest name I know;
Fills my every longing, Keeps me singing as I go."

The third stanza pointed to the past, for in it the poet-preacher sang:

"Though sometimes he leads through waters deep, Trials fall
     across the way,
Though sometimes the path seems rough and steep,
See his footprints all the way."

And the last looked to the future:

"Soon He's coming back to welcome me, Far beyond the starry
     sky,
I shall wing my flight to worlds unknown, I shall reign with Him
     on high."

In 1914 Luther Bridgers became a General Evangelist of his Church, conducting services throughout the length and breadth of American Methodism for the next eighteen years except for a brief period following World War I when he helped establish missions in Belgium and Czeckoslovakia and aided Church rehabilitation in Russia. That same year he was united in marriage with Miss Aline Winburn of Gainesville, Georgia, a former head of the Conservatory of Shorter College, Rome, Georgia, a talented musician who travelled with her husband and provided the instrumental accompaniments for his song services for the next three decades. To their union a son, named for his distinguished father, was born, who, at this writing in 1959, resides in Atlanta.

From 1932 until 1945 he served as pastor of several Churches in Georgia and North Carolina. His pastoral appointments included three Atlanta Methodist Churches, Trinity, Inman Park and Haygood Memorial. In 1944 he transferred to the North Carolina Conference, serving the congregation at Morehead City until his retirement the following year, whereupon he made his home in Gainesville, Georgia, continuing to serve as an evangelist where needed. The last six months of his life saw him on a special mission for Bishop Arthur Moore at Palatka, Florida.

At the age of 64, the veteran preacher, evangelist, Mason, song-leader, poet and song-writer, passed away in an Atlanta hospital, May 27, 1948, being buried two days later in the Alta Vista Cemetery, Gainesville. His widow wrote, "To me he was the finest expression of what the Holy Spirit could do through a man in his preaching when he strives at all times to honor the Holy Spirit.

In his preaching he was fearless, and in leading souls to Christ he was irresistible."

His Memoir, prepared by Rev. Dr. William P. King, for the North Carolina Conference of 1948, contained this significant sentence, "God does not measure life by length of years but by depth of devotion, and height of purpose and breadth of compassion." By all three standards, Luther Burgess Bridgers had been "a good minister of Jesus Christ", to whose glory he today is undoubtedly continuing to sing his songs of praise and love.

10.

HIS EYE IS ON THE SPARROW

One mid-summer Sunday morning in the mid nineteen-forties, just as I began preaching to my congregation at the Methodist Church in Madison Heights, Virginia, a sparrow flew into the Church sanctuary through an open window and proceeded to "break up" the service by flying about in obviously confused and frantic distraction, in a vain effort to get back out into the open air again. After trying to compete with the sparrow for a few moments, I gave up and sat down until the exhausted little bird finally landed atop one of the organ pipes not too far from where I was sitting, from which vantage point he kept an "eagle eye" on the congregation until I had finished my sermon, announced the closing hymn, pronounced the benediction and gone home.

When I returned for the evening service, the sparrow was nowhere to be found. Where or how or when he had made his exit remained forever a mystery.

The next morning, when the Methodist ministers gathered for their regular Monday morning "bull session", I told the brethren what had happened. One of the pastors present immediately spoke up and said, "Ernest, why didn't you change your sermon on the spur of the moment and preach on 'The Fifth Sparrow'?"

I replied, " 'The fifth sparrow?' What about it?"

The other minister explained, "In Matthew 10:29, Jesus said, 'Are not two sparrows sold for a farthing (a penny)? And not one of them will fall to the ground without your Father's will.' But in another account of that saying of the Lord, found in Luke 12:6, the author of the third Gospel wrote that the Master said, 'Are not five sparrows sold for two farthings (pennies)? And not one of them is forgotten by God.' "

Then he continued, "You see, the poor people of Jesus' day bought sparrows for food. Two sparrows sold for one penny, while, for two pennies, you not only got four sparrows but a fifth one thrown in for good measure, as an extra, or a bonus. But even that poor, neglected, forgotten fifth sparrow was known to the Heavenly Father."

I smiled and said, "I only wish I had had that idea last Monday instead of today. I might have made a pretty good sermon of 'The Fifth Sparrow'." The fact that Jesus had said many times to his followers "You are of more value than many sparrows" comforted untold numbers of believers during the first twenty centuries of the Christian era. Among those who found "solace, strength and rest" in those words was a saintly invalid, Mrs. Doolittle by name, who lived with her devoted husband in the city of Elmira, New York shortly after the close of the nineteenth century.

It has been reported that Mrs. Doolittle was bedridden for more than two decades, during much of which time her husband suffered as an "incurable cripple", managing his business affairs as well as handling his domestic duties from a wheel chair. Yet, in spite of such handicaps, that would have crushed the spirits of less stalwart souls, both Mr. and Mrs. Doolittle lived "happy Christian lives" that proved to be sources of inspiration and comfort to all who came within their influence.

It was in the early spring of 1905 that another couple was introduced to the Doolittles, as a result of which a fast friendship developed between the four consecrated Christians. Dr. and Mrs. W. Stillman Martin, well-known as Baptist evangelists and singers, met the Doolittles during their stay in the New York community, and immediately recognized the unusual radiance which both husband and wife possessed.

Mrs. Martin, a native of Nova Scotia, where she had been born on August 21, 1867, had married the Baptist clergyman, who was five years her senior, and, turning her back upon a school teacher's career, became his travelling companion and co-worker during his extensive evangelistic tours. At his insistence, she continued to write and publish under her maiden initials, signing her prose and poetry "Mrs. C. D. Martin" instead of "Mrs. W. S. Martin".

On one of their visits to the Doolittle home in Elmira, the evangelist commented upon the radiance and cheerfulness of their host and his invalid wife. Curiously, he asked them to reveal the secret of their "holy joy". The wife's reply was as beautiful as it was brief, and as Scriptural as it was simple. She graciously answered her guest by saying, "His eye is on the sparrow and I know He watches me".

Mrs. Martin instantly saw the possibilities in that phrase, and, before the day came to a close, she had embellished it and arranged her lines and phrases in poetic form. In her opening stanza she asked a number of questions, like those the Doolittles must have asked themselves a hundred times before resolving them and finding the answers in their own hearts:

"Why should I feel discouraged, Why should the shadows come? Why should my heart be lonely And long for Heaven and home?"

She discovered her answer in the words of Mrs. Doolittle, "His eye is on the sparrow and I know He watches me". For that reason alone could she write, in the chorus, "I sing because I'm happy, I sing because I'm free", since only those who know God as Jesus revealed Him can be happy or free.

Like Rev. John Henry Newman, who, in his autobiographical hymn "Lead Kindly Light" used the phrase "one step enough for me", Mrs. Martin, in her second stanza expressed a similar sentiment, "Though by the path He leadeth, But one step I may see", but her heart refused to be troubled since the God who watched the sparrow also had his loving eye upon her.

It only remained for one man named Charles to compose a suitable tune and another man named Charles to sing it, and the song was on its way to well-merited fame. The composer was Iowa-born Charles H. Gabriel (1856-1932) who had once promised his mother that he would one day write a song that would become famous. He lived to see hundreds of his tunes become the "popular songs" of his day, among them "The Awakening

Chorus", "Send The Light", "The Way Of The Cross Leads Home", "He Is So Precious to Me" as well as "His Eye Is On The Sparrow" and many, many more. Some of them brought him plenty of popularity but no money, while others sold for as little as two dollars and a half or as much as five dollars.

At the height of his creative powers he turned out a variety of music, including cantatas, anthems, collections for male voices as well as women's voices, gospel song-books, children's hymnals and books to teach other people how to teach still others how to read music as well as sing it.

The quality as well as the quantity of his compositions must have brought joy to the heart of his Mother, who had told him on one occasion that she would rather have him write a song that would help somebody else than be president of the United States.

The singer was none other than Charles M. Alexander who introduced Mrs. Martin's new stanzas and Gabriel's new tune to an English audience during an evangelistic tour of Great Britain in company with the renowned preacher, Dr. Torrey.

Since that initial presentation, "His Eye Is On The Sparrow" has grown in popularity, until it is known and loved wherever the Gospel has been preached. In fact, a famous colored actress selected that phrase as the title for her autobiography since she felt that it so perfectly and completely described the story of her life. That thousands of other devout believers have felt the same way is the testimony of Christians the world over, and the certainty that God, who knows the first, second, third, fourth and even the fifth sparrow, values us much more than the sparrows, has become the precious conviction of those who have found His true nature through the revelation of Himself in His Son, Jesus Christ, Our Lord.

11.

HOW GREAT THOU ART

One of the several hundred religious organizations now active in the United States is the church group known as the Evangelical Mission Covenant Church of America. In 1956 this body reported a membership of more than fifty-three thousand people divided into slightly more than five-hundred separate congregations. The Church originated in Sweden as a protest against the strict formalism of the Lutheran Church, which is the established state church of that Scandinavian country.

This "free church" group was brought to the United States about 1885 and was for many years known as the Swedish Evangelical Mission Covenant Church of America. Today their adherent accept and use the Apostles' Creed as a statement of faith, practice only two sacraments, baptism and the Lord's supper, and have national headquarters in Chicago, where they have established North Park College and a Theological Seminary for the training of their ministers. Missionaries are being sent to several foreign countries, while here at home the members support homes for the aged, orphanages, hospitals and several educational institutions.

The 1950 edition of the official Hymnal of this denomination contained a hymn which was in reality a translation by Professor E. Gustav Johnson of North Park College, entitled "O Mighty God", made by him in 1925, and first published in an official hymn book six years later, in 1931. Professor Johnson made his translation from an original Swedish poem which had been penned in 1886 by Carl Boberg (1859-1940).

Boberg's poem of praise was actually a record of God's mighty works as the poet had observed them in the world about him, for in his poem he mentioned the stars above, the rolling thunder of the heavens, the mysterious woods and forests of his native land as well as other beauties and glories of nature, climaxing his adoration of the Creator by giving thanks for His noblest gift, that of His only Son "who suffered and died to take away our sin".

Boberg's poem had been published in one or two periodicals in Sweden and then apparently forgotten. But someone noticed that the metrical pattern of the new stanzas was identical with that of an old familiar Swedish folk song, and quickly substituted the new words for the old ones, and, before his death, Boberg had the satisfaction of hearing his hymn sung to the simple but moving melody of a tune that had become one of the cherished possessions of his people.

Undoubtedly the original poet well knew the Old Testament prophecy contained in Isaish 9:6, in which the coming Messiah was spoken of as "Wonderful Counsellor, the Mighty God, the Everlasting Father, the Prince of Peace", and took the phrase "Mighty God" directly from that verse, although the Old Testament was filled with many references to God as a "Mighty One".

Strangely enough, "O Mighty God" did not remain in Sweden nor in the native tongue of poet Boberg. Before the poet knew it, the stanzas were translated into many "foreign tongues" including Russian, Polish and German, in the process of which some of his words and phrases were altered to conform to the thought-patterns and expressions of the languages into which they were translated, while the translations mirrored the spiritual experiences of the translators as well as that of the man who had written the original in Sweden years before.

Among those who discovered the hymn in its Russian rendition was a native of London, England, who was serving as a missionary in the Ukraine during the years 1923-1939, Rev. Stuart K. Hine. Unaware of Boberg's original or of Johnson's English translation, Hine credited the impressive version to a Russian prisoner, dating it as far back as 1921, and immediately decided to make an English translation of a hymn he considered a noble Russian affirmation of Christian faith. As a result of his labors, "O Mighty God" became "How Great Thou Art" as it was distilled through the hearts and minds of the many intermediaries through whom the poem had passed in the intervening decades.

Hine was on firm Scriptural grounds, however, in speaking and singing of the greatness of God, for the Bible abounds in references to God's great love (Psalm 86:13), His great works (Psalms 92:5), His great mercy, (Psalm 119:156), His great glory (Psalm 138:5), His great understanding (Proverbs 14:29) and His personal greatness (Psalm 35:27; Psalm 70:4).

Richard M. Elmer, Director of Music at Cleveland Bible College, communicated with Rev. Mr. Hine, and received from him a letter in which Hine detailed the various steps involved in his discovery and translation of the Russian version of Boberg's hymn of thanksgiving and praise. In his version Hine, unaware that the hymn in another form had already appeared in a denominational hymnal, changed "O Mighty God" to "How Great Thou Art", but he conformed to the spirit of the original when he spoke of standing in "awesome wonder" before the majesty of the Creator's work in the star-studded heavens above as well as on the earth below, with its wooded mountains and its "forest glades", its brooks and its breezes that all bespeak their Maker's wondrous power and give evidence of His matchless glory.

Hine's translation, made in 1948, became almost immediately popular when it was picked up and used as a sacred solo by one of the singers associated with the Billy Graham evangelistic team, during the middle decade of the twentieth century. The "natural" melody and harmonies of the "Chorus" strongly resemble some of the phrases in W. H. Doane's tune for Fanny Crosby's popular gospel hymn "Pass me not, O gentle Saviour" and are reminiscent of the Hawaiian national song "Aloha", showing that singers in all lands tend to express themselves in the same musical idioms as their poets do in using similar figures of speech.

Now available in popular sheet music form, "How Great Thou Art" has captured the fancy of the church-going public. If those who sing it will remember that in every land there are fellow believers who still stand in awe of the greatness of God, and that every true hymn of thanksgiving and praise knows no national or ecclesiastical barriers or boundaries, the ministry of this hymn will have had its rich reward.

Since any folk melody lends itself to a wide variety of harmonizations by musicians of many different cultures, the music of Boberg's hymn has undergone many changes in its harmonic structure, while the original melody has remained constant. As such, it will continue to serve as a reminder that all of God's creatures

50

stand in need of His great love and are the unworthy recipients of His great mercy, and as often as citizens of different climes and tongues sing it, "How Great Thou Art" will continue to be another "golden cord, close-binding all mankind".

12.

I BELONG TO THE KING

It all began when Miss Ida L. Reed was reading a copy of the "Christian Herald" magazine many years ago back in her little hillside home on a sparsely cultivated piece of rocky, rough farmland near Philippi, West Virginia. Ida's life had not been a particularly happy one, what with stark poverty staring her family in the face at every turn and her own body being ravaged by one disease after another. Fifteen years after her birth on November 30, 1865, an epidemic of the worst kind of diphtheria broke out in her section of the West Virginia hills. Those who died were considered more fortunate than those who lived the rest of their lives in semi-blindness and partial invalidism following their long and slow recovery from the dread disease.

Ida Reed was one of those who "recovered" but never forgot that particular epidemic. Her long and slow recuperation was made all the more painful because the untimely death of her tubercular father threw a great deal of the burden of running the farm as well as assisting with the housework upon her tiny shoulders. When her mother broke down under the weight of so much woe, Ida looked after her with loving and tender care, and when Mrs. Reed died, Ida stayed right there in her humble mountain home, carrying on as best she could under such trying circumstances. Then it was that the religious journal, "Christian Herald", began its wonder-working miracle in her lonely life.

To while away the hours during her days of painful illness, or to seek solace and strength after a trying day doing the chores as well as struggling to eke out an existence from the barren soil that made up most of the family farm, she began to lose herself in the articles, poems, sermons and stories of this wonderful magazine.

A serial entitled "A Princess in Calico", which appeared in some of the issues close to the end of the first decade of the twentieth century, was especially appealing and Ida could hardly wait for the mails to bring the next chapter of the thrilling story after she had finished the chapter in the current issue. One phrase of one character never left her memory, the character being a little girl, and the phrase, her words in reply to a questioner who had asked her how she could smile and be happy in the midst of so many trials and tribulations, "Oh, it's because I belong to the King!" Little did the half-sick farm girl dream that some years later those words would inspire her to write a poem that many Circles of King's Daughters would adopt as their very own, and which would eventually become a popular gospel song that would appear in more than thirty-five different hymnals and songbooks, with an estimated sale of over four-million copies.

As soon as her strength returned, Ida Reed began to teach in a nearby district school, and, to help her pupils learn new songs, she wrote her own words to several familiar tunes. When her brother pointed out that in a religious paper he was reading the poems and songs were no better than Ida's initial efforts, she tried her hand at writing original poems, and to her surprise, learned that the editor of the magazine not only liked her poems but wanted to buy and publish them. The money was nothing to speak of, but a dollar here and two dollars there went a long way toward balancing the family budget, and soon Ida Reed was writing more poems and finding more publishers eager to purchase her works and publish them. An editor of some Sunday School periodicals in Pittsburgh, Pennsylvania liked her "appealing verses" and asked her to write regularly for some of his publications. By the time she was twenty-three, she was receiving tunes in the mail, and sending back her own stanzas in return.

Still the unspoiled country girl, Ida Reed's life began to touch the lives of the leading song-writers of her day, and soon she was corresponding with such notables as Ira D. Sankey, who composed the tune for "The Ninety and Nine", and Fanny Crosby, the remarkable poetic genius who wrote more than eight-thousand poems in her ninety-five years, as well as Hart Pease Danks, who composed the music for "No Night There" and "Silver Threads Among The Gold."

During her long nights of pain-wracked sleeplessness, she used to think out her poems, calling them her "songs in the night", concentrating upon them "to save herself from sinking into unconsciousness or delerium". Mr. George Sanville is the authority for the fact that it was during a period of suffering and sickness while Miss Reed was bed-ridden in a hospital in Washington, D.C. that the words of the little girl in the "Christian Herald" serial came back into her mind. From her hospital bed she began to write about the King of her heart, and His Kingdom, in these simple and moving lines:

> "I belong to the King, I'm a child of His love,
> I shall dwell in His palace so fair;
> For He tells of its bliss in yon heaven above,
> And His Children its splendors shall share.

Chorus

> I belong to the King, I'm a child of His love,
> And He never forsaketh His own;
> He will call me some day to His palace above,
> I shall dwell by His glorified throne."

Her subsequent stanzas speak of her conviction that God loves her and is still her "refuge unfailing", and her willingness to claim His "exceeding great and precious promises" to undergird her during the trials of this life.

When Maurice Clifton set her poem to music, its future was assured, and the invalid's song soon sang its melodious way throughout the Christian world. Twenty-five years after "A Princess in Calico" was printed, Beatrice Plumb wrote a series of articles for the same magazine, entitled "Hymns We Love to Sing". Among the letters she received as a result of her interesting stories was one from a seventy-five year old woman who still resided in the hills of West Virginia, and who introduced herself to the author by asking her if she knew the gospel song "I Belong to the King". Confessing that it was one of her own songs, Ida L. Reed told the story of the writing of many other hymns, and, telling of her continued "lack and loneliness", said, "I shall never, in all probability, have enough to take away the dread of my tomorrows, or the shadow of my last days, but I am deeply grateful that God let me do my humble best for the Kingdom."

Miss Plumb told the story of Ida L. Reed in the "Christian Herald" of March, 1940, with the result that individuals, groups and organizations from far and wide wrote in offering financial help as well as strength and skill to make the seventy-four year old song-writer's last years beautiful and carefree.

Earlier, in the November 26, 1939 issue of The Wheeling (West Virginia) Intelligencer, under the date line "Philippi, West Virginia", an article told the reading public of the desperate plight of the woman who had written more than two-thousand gospel songs during her tragic and triumphant life. The reporter who prepared the story, Mr. Herman G. Johnson, said to a correspondent, "Frankly, I did not describe her condition anyways near as bad as it really is. Without family and few neighbours, she is living alone on a side road three miles from the main highway. She has a cow, a few chickens and cultivates a small garden." Upon being notified of this matter by interested friends and individuals, The American Society of Composers, Authors and Publishers (ASCAP) voted Miss Ida L. Reed a monthly grant for the rest of her life "in appreciation for her substantial contribution to religious music", a stipend they were happy to send her from December 1939 until her death on July 8, 1951, at the age of eighty-five, when the poet and hymn-writer, worn with the toil of eight and a half decades, claimed the promise of the King of Kings, as she had sung of them in the last stanza of her most popular gospel song:

> "I belong to the King, and His promise is sure,
> That we all shall be gathered at last,
> In His Kingdom above, by life's waters so pure
> When this life with its trials is past."

13.

I NEED JESUS

By strange and devious paths the stories that inspired many of our finest hymns and most popular gospel songs come to light. When this writer was delivering a series of addresses on "Practical Hymnology" to the Methodist ministers of the Pacific Northwest at the College of Puget Sound in Tacoma, Washington, one of the local pastors asked him if he knew of the thrilling story back of the writing of the gospel song "Tis so sweet to trust in Jesus". When I confessed my ignorance, he referred me to a missionary in Southern Rhodesia, Africa, and, after correspondence with him, the true and dramatic story of Mrs. Louisa M. R. Stead, the author of that gospel song, was brought to my attention, and included as one of the fifty true "living stories" in my recent book, "Favorite Stories of Inspiring Hymns".

Then, during a missionary conference at Lake Junaluska, N.C., the Methodist Assembly Ground, the wife of a minister of an Atlanta church asked me to find for her the history of the sacred poem "In the secret of his presence", for which the well-known composer, Goerge Stebbins, had composed the music many years ago. To find out about the author, a noble Christian woman who was a native of India, I had to borrow some books from the British Missionary Society, and dig out the fascinating facts from those volumes, and this true story, too, is included as one of the fifty chapters in the afore-mentioned collection of "living stories".

Stranger still is the fact that a published review of this new book brought to light the story behind another well-known gospel song by an unusual and yet providential chain of circumstances.

A correspondent from Battle Creek, Michigan, wrote to me to this effect, "Recently in a folder from the Sunshine Magazine, I came across your name. It has brought many memories back to me. When I was about seven years old, my father had a pastorate in Watervliet, New York, and it was at that time that a Rev. Emurian came to help Dad in a project that was dear to his heart. He opened his church, for many Armenian people had recently settled in that vicinity and needed a place to worship and to fellowship together. As I remember, my father and this Rev. Emurian became fast friends. They had a mutual love for music and hymns. If my memory hasn't played me wrong, I think they worked on some together. Dad was Rev. George W. Webster, who wrote 'The victory may depend on you', 'He took my place', and 'I need Jesus'. His last pastorate was twenty years in the Federated Church of Essex, New York. Dad left us in October of 1942 but still lives through his songs."

When I mentioned this letter to my parents, they both immediately recalled with great interest the visits that Rev. George Orlia Webster (1866-1942) had paid to our home when my father, Rev. S. K. Emurian, was pastor of the Presbyterian Church in Fort Edward, New York, during the years from 1913 until 1918. Mother particularly remembered the way my brother and I would look forward to Mr. Webster's visits and the fellowship all of us enjoyed around the table at meal time in the Fort Edward Presbyterian manse.

"He would often ask little Helene to sing what he called 'The Prayer Hymn'," Mother added, "and little sister, who was then not over two-and-a-half years of age, would climb up on a kitchen chair, throw her little head back and sing the stately cadences of 'Holy, Holy, Holy, Lord God Almighty', although she stumbled over Bishop Heber's words many times, and seldom knew what she was singing about." But Mr. Webster would smile and applaud and congratulate the little girl on the accuracy of her rendition. Little Helene passed away at the age of ten in 1925, and doubtless, as a charming young lady, she and saintly old George Orlia Webster are singing together the praises of God in "the sweet bye and bye".

Father often invited Webster to fill his pulpit in the little upper New York State town not far from famed Hudson Falls and Glens Falls, and within traveling distance of beautiful Lake George, and if he happened to be called away suddenly on some pressing personal or church matter, he would ask Mother, "Who shall I get to preach next Sunday morning?" and mother would usually say, "Why not ask George Webster? Our people like to hear him preach, and our three children love to have him as a guest in our home."

So it was that the writer of more than two thousand gospel songs came into the life of the Emurian family before any of the three children were old enough to appreciate him or to properly evaluate the contribution he was making to gospel hymnody. But in addition to the fact that they were both ministers, he and my distinguished father had a tie that bound their hearts and lives together, because Webster was a fluent poet and Emurian was a gifted musician, singer and composer. When I asked Webster's daughter, Mrs. Mabel Webster Palmer, of Michigan, to tell me more about her father's life, ministry and gospel songs, she graciously obliged and closed her letter with this request "Does your father still have a copy of the Clericus Song written so long ago? His music and Dad's words."

Mother dug out the old scrap book and looked through the yellowed clippings of bygone years, and suddenly, with a cry of joy, handed me a copy of "The Clericus Hymn" with words by George Orlia Webster and music by S. K. Emurian. Written for an association of thirty-five ministers of Glens Falls, New York and vicinity, the hymn was copyrighted and published in 1915 by the Tullar-Meredith Company. Webster's first stanza contained these lines:

> Thy servants, Lord, before thee stand, Thy will to know.
> The service which for each is planned, Or high or low;
> We would not dare to choose our task, But wait thy word;
> Thy will, thy will alone, we ask, Thou art our Lord.

One day, during his long pastorate at Essex, New York, Webster was sitting on the parsonage steps when he saw a man reeling out of a place that was called "The Coffee Cup" although it was more of a tavern than a restaurant. Realizing that the man was drunk, Webster said to himself, "That man needs Jesus", and just as suddenly followed that phrase with the sequel, "How much more do I need Jesus in order to help that man." Rising from the parsonage porch, he went into the study in which he prepared his sermons and wrote his hymns and songs for a score of years, and began to write:

"I need Jesus; my need I now confess,
No friend like Him in times of deep distress;
I need Jesus, the need I gladly own.
Though some may bear their load alone, Yet I need Jesus.

Chorus:

I need Jesus, I need Jesus, I need Jesus every day;
Need him in the sunshine hour, need Him when the storm clouds
    lower,
Every day, along my way, Yes, I need Jesus."

Later Charles Gabriel set those three stanzas and chorus to music, and gave Christendom the gospel hymn that brought many needy souls to the foot of the cross.

After his death on October 1, 1942, at the age of seventy-six, one of Webster's daughters wrote to the other, "I always think of how perfectly beautiful it was that day when Daddy went. It always seemed so right, somehow, that he should have gone on when the earth he loved so was so beautiful — as if the banners had been flying out in his honor." In that way did the man who wrote "I Need Jesus" march out to meet His Lord, who now had need of him!

14.

I WANT TO BE AN ANGEL

The talented Warner Sisters were so hesitant about submitting their first original novels to the publishers of their day that each girl sent her works under a pen name. The eldest sister, Susan Warner (1819-1885) became "Elizabeth Wetherell" while Anna (1822-1915) the youngest, adopted the name "Amy Lothrop". Neither sister felt she had a natural bent for writing successful prose, and they turned to their literary pursuits only after the death of their mother and the business failure of their father compelled them to try their hands at something creative in order to supplement the family income.

Their father, Henry W. Warner, Esquire, a well-to-do New York lawyer, lost nearly everything he had in the financial panic of 1837, and was compelled to sell his luxurious Long Island home in order to satisfy some of his creditors. Fortunately that loss did not leave him entirely homeless. The previous year, while visiting his brother Thomas, the Chaplain as well as Professor of Geography, History and Ethics at the United States Military Academy, West Point, New York, he had seen and then purchased what was known at that time as Constitution Island, buying it from Mr. and Mrs. Samuel Gouvernier on November 3, 1836. Prior to that sale, the valuable and strategically located island had been in the hands of the Philips' family as part of a Crown grant.

On this historic site of the first military fortification on the Hudson River dating back to 1776, Mr. Warner erected a lovely home, which he named "Wood Crag". His wife having passed away several years earlier, Mr. Warner persuaded his sister Fanny to come to Constitution Island and make a home there for him and his two growing girls, Susan and Anna. Under her guidance and tutelage, the girls were able to make the transition from a life of wealth, culture and luxury to one of careful budgeting, less of the social whirl, and more of practical and creative work. Looking back upon those days after she had established herself as a successful author, Susan said, "We left home, silk and satin dresses, carriage house and servants to don calico and to do work with our hands that we had always considered menial."

But had it not been for that change of atmosphere the sisters would hardly have taken up the task of writing the books and poems by which they are remembered and for which they are admired and loved to this very day. Nineteen year old Susan, the musician of the family, and fifteen year old Anna, the delicate introspective adolescent, tried their hands at a wide variety of things, from making flags to making ceramics until, encouraged and prodded by Aunt Fanny, they began to write a book. When the daring work was finally completed, Susan balanced her budget and discovered that she had sixty-three dollars in the bank to pay debts that amounted to more than one-hundred dollars. But her book, "The Wide, Wide World", found a sympathetic reader in the person of the mother of George Putnam, the head of the publishing company that bore his family name, and at her insistence,

Putnam published the book, which became a sensational best-seller, being out-sold only by Harriet Beecher Stowe's "Uncle Tom's Cabin". Thrilled by the fame and fortune that Susan's first book brought, the two Warner sisters embarked upon a literary career that saw them writing more than seventy books during their times. Some of these were written by Susan, and some by Anna, while several of the best were the results of sisterly collaboration.

In 1859, their novel, "Say and Seal", was published in two parts. The demand for this book became so great that a one-volume, one thousand page edition was printed the very next year, 1860, in the preface of which both "Elizabeth Wetherell" and "Amy Lothrop" confessed that it was a joint undertaking. The story of Faith Derrick, John Endecott Linden, Johnny Fax and the other fictional characters became an overnight best-seller. But, little did either sister dream that long after the last printing of the book, a poem in Volume I and another in Volume II, would be remembered and sung by generations of children the world over, in many climes and tongues far removed from the safety and security of Constitution Island and West Point. On page 129 of the 1860 one-volume edition of this novel, loaned this writer by the Enoch Pratt Library of Baltimore, the Warner sisters have Faith and Mr. Linden accompany a group of boys from their Sunday School on an outing, little Johnny Fax sitting in his accustomed place on Mr. Linden's lap. As the two older people are enjoying the beauties of God's great out-of-doors, the silence is broken suddenly as the boys begin singing a familiar hymn. After a moment, Mr. Linden joins with them in singing:

I want to be an angel, And with the angels stand,
A crown upon my forehead, A harp within my hand;
There, right before my Saviour, So glorious and so bright,
I'd make the sweetest music, And praise him day and night.

I never should be weary, Nor ever shed a tear,
Nor ever know a sorrow, Nor ever feel a fear;
But blessed, pure and holy, I'd dwell in Jesus' sight,
And with ten thousand thousand, Praise him both day and night.

Set to music soon after its first appearance in the pages of this popular novel, "I Want To Be An Angel" became the favorite of

Sunday School children throughout the English speaking world, and was quickly translated into several foreign tongues and carried to the far corners of Christendom by the missionaries who girdled the globe with the Gospel of Jesus and His love.

In 1891, when my grandfather, Rev. Harutune S. Jenanyan, took his wife and little daughter on a perilous and dangerous missionary journey from Tarsus, Asia Minor, the city of St. Paul, to Sivas in Armenia, they travelled on horse-back through robber-infested country for fourteen days. Two of the leading robber chiefs in that territory, were Chollo, whose "name cast terror on every side" since he had successfully evaded pursuing Government forces for many months, and Kara Agha, a famous Koorish chief, whose name caused even the fearsome Chollo to tremble. Harutune took his small party directly into the heart of Kara Agha's country, telling those he met enroute that he was going to be Agha's guest in his own village. When they reached the brigand's head-quarters, the missionary asked that they be received as guests for the night. The surprised robber chief gave them accommodations, entertaining Harutune in his own spacious tent while his wife, Helene, and their little daughter, Grace, were cared for in another tent by the women of the village. The next morning, before taking their leave, the missionary asked for permission to read a portion of the Holy Scripture, and then offered a prayer. Seeing that the chief was somewhat affected, he then said, "Do you wish to have the little child sing for you?" The chief replied, "Oh, yes; can she?" Then little Grace, only three-and-a-half years old, came forward and stood before the tall old man and sang two songs she had recently learned in the Sunday School in Tarsus, singing them in the native tongue, "Jesus loves me, this I know" and "I want to be an angel". The chief was so deeply touched, that he sent his own son, Bekkeer Agha, mounted on a handsome Arabian steed, to lead the small missionary party through the rest of his territory.

So the Jenanyans and their escorts travelled safely with Bekkeer at the head of their caravan, until they reached the security of the city of Sivas. Little Grace, who is my mother, remembers rather vaguely that eventful trip many years ago, but she can still sing in her native tongue the stanzas of the hymn with which she charmed the robber chief many years ago. Small wonder, then, that the stanzas are precious to her and her family. The words of the last two stanzas, as the Warner sisters wrote them in 1859, are still dear to her heart:

I know I'm weak and sinful, But Jesus will forgive,
For many little children, Have gone to heaven to live.
Dear Saviour, when I languish, And lay me down to die,
Oh, send a shining angel, To bear me to the sky!

Oh, there, I'll be an angel, And with the angels stand!
A crown upon my forehead, A harp within my hand.
And there before my Saviour, So glorious and so bright,
I'll make the sweetest music, And praise him day and night!

15.

IF YOUR HEART KEEPS RIGHT

There is an appropriate verse in the Bible to fit every individual, and each person can find in the Holy Scripture a verse or phrase that provides an accurate description of every different type of character and personality, proving that the Sacred Word is still a perfect mirror of God's proudest creation, man.

A few days after Mrs. Clarence Dickinson (1875-1957) died in New York in August, 1957, a memorial service in her honor was held in The Brick Church in that great city where she had served with great distinction as organist for nearly half a century. In "The Memorial Tribute" prepared for that occasion, the writer suggested that there were four verbs which told the story of this remarkable musician-composer's life. Referring to Matthew 28:6-7, in which the Angel at the open tomb on the first Easter morning said to the frightened women, "He is not here for He is risen, even as He said, Come, see the place where the Lord lay; And go quickly and tell His disciples", the writer stated that the four verbs, "Come, See, Go, Tell" summed up the life, influence and creative musical ministry of Helen Dickinson, and a finer tribute to a faithful Christian would be almost impossible to find.

In like manner, the life of another heroine of the Cross, Mrs. Lizzie DeArmond, was a living illustration of the text found in I John 4:4, "Little children you are of God and have overcome them; for he who is in you is greater than he who is in the world". Had it not been for that fact, the life of this Godly woman would have been merely a record of sorrow piled upon sorrow and tragedy heaped upon tragedy. However, with the spirit of the living Lord in her heart, she experienced "the victory that overcomes the world".

While some poor misguided individuals try to ignore their troubles in the vain hope that by turning their backs upon misfortune, she will soon disappear, Mrs. DeArmond faced hers in the confident assurance of God's guiding and protecting presence.

And, whereas some people stoically resign themselves to the cruel arrows of outrageous fortune, this noble housewife and mother accepted them, and overcame them in the spirit of Rev. Johnson Oatman, Jr. who wrote in his hymn "Higher Ground", these lines, "I want to live above the world, Though Satan's darts at me are hurled."

When the new Presbyterian Sunday School in Swarthmore, Pa. was organized Mrs. DeArmond served as a faithful teacher in the Primary Department, working in this capacity until "she was too old to travel back and forth" from her home to the Church. The radiant light of her Christian faith never shone more beautifully or brilliantly than during the days when one of her daughters was very sick. In the presence of diseases and epidemics which take such a huge toll of human life, even sincere believers stand hushed and helpless, knowing not what the future holds for lover or for loved one. But Mrs. DeArmond did more than that. She dared to stare death in the face and say to the grim reaper, "If I must say 'Goodnight' here, someone else will be saying 'Good morning' up there." With that phrase in mind, she penned the three stanzas and chorus of her gospel song "Goodnight and Good morning", in which she spoke of the blessed release that comes to the weary who pass from the cares and woes of this life to Christ's kingdom of peace over on the other side, and, catching a glimpse of the light of God shining in the face of Christ Jesus, her Lord, she sang of the wonderful love of such a Saviour who permits us to share his heaven with him.

Her married life was spent in Swarthmore, and it was there that she made a home for her husband and their children. As early as her eighth year, though, she had written articles for publication, and, for a while, conducted a question and answer column in a newspaper under the name "Dinah". Her sweet singing voice, coupled with an innate talent for music, caused her to be in much demand in many local Churches. When she was left alone to support her large family, she picked up her pencil and pen once again and began to turn out hymns and recitations and special programs for use in Sunday Schools throughout the country.

Her daughter, Miss Linda DeArmond, who celebrated her eighty-first birthday in 1957, wrote of her mother in these moving words, "Her life was a hard struggle but she was always cheerful and happy." Then, explaining that "it took a lot of hymn writing to supply food for the children," she told how her mother received as little as $1, or as much as $2 and even $5 for her sacred poems, adding, "Just when things would almost give out, a small check would come in and she always said the Lord provided."

It was her faith in the power of prayer that inspired Mrs. De-Armond to pen the three stanzas of her gospel song, "Mother's Prayers Have Followed Me", for which Mr. B. D. Ackley composed the music in 1912, and it is not hard to believe that a saintly woman who could be calm in the face of death could also find little difficulty in believing in the wonderful power of intercessory prayer. It was also in 1912 that Mrs. DeArmond wrote the stanzas of her most famous gospel song, "If Your Heart Keeps Right", for which Mr. Ackley also composed a lilting tune.

The composer confirmed the date of authorship as 1912, but added that it was fast becoming one of the favorites prior to the Billy Sunday Philadelphia campaign which opened in the City of Brotherly Love in January of 1915, a series of services with which the song has been closely identified. It was in these stanzas that the poet saw "blossoms of gladness" growing beneath the snow of winter, and saw the promise of morning's glow lurking behind every dark and gloomy cloud. Here it was that she sang of "joy for the taking", and explained how, in her own life, she had conquered toil and care by bearing other people's burdens, and "making their lives bright", closing each stanza with the familiar admonition, which had been forged on the anvil of her own experience, "Every cloud will wear a rainbow, if your heart keeps right."

So intrigued were her publishers with this catchy phrase that the Rodeheaver Company accepted it, and copyrighted it, using the words to adorn all of their stationery and many of their publications, printing the musical staff in the shape of a rainbow.

At the time of her death, those who knew her best agreed that the gospel songwriter of Swarthmore, in the words of the closing stanza of her most popular sacred poem, had gained "the rest of the victor" because she had never given up the struggle but had won the fight, since on account of her virile faith in a loving God her own heart had been kept right.

16.

IT PAYS TO SERVE JESUS

During the fourth week in September, 1958, while I was conducting a series of Hymn Festivals in the First Methodist Church of Jacksonville, Florida, it was my privilege to meet a remarkable brother minister who was also a well-known musician and hymnwriter, Rev. Frank C. Huston, who had celebrated his eighty-seventh birthday the previous week. Because of my interest in and my love for the fine gospel hymns of the Christian faith, Brother Huston's name was not a new one to me, for I had been singing some of his finest tunes for many years in Sunday School and Church gatherings, and some of the fondest recollections of my childhood included my distinguished father's playing and singing of several of Huston's best-known compositions. I was surprised to note how cheerful and radiant the octogenarian appeared when he came forward at the close of one of my services and introduced himself to me. After a warm handclasp, he insisted upon presenting me with an autographed copy of his own book "One Hundred Hymns and Gospel Songs", whereupon I was equally insistent that he accept from me an autographed copy of one of my recent publications, "Living Stories of Famous Hymns".

When I returned to my parish in Portsmouth, Virginia at the close of the Florida services, we engaged in quite a lengthy correspondence, during which Mr. Huston was kind enough to tell me some of the interesting facts about his own long life and fruitful ministry, as well as some of the fascinating incidents that inspired him to write several of his most popular sacred songs. He was a native of Indiana, he told me, having been born in the town of Orange in Fayette County on September 12, 1871. His inherited musical talent revealed itself at a very early age, his parents later confessing that Frank "could whistle a tune before he could talk". At twelve he was playing the cornet in a brass concert band, and at seventeen he was dividing his time between singing in a popular male quartet and directing the congregational singing for revival services in the surrounding territory. The next few years were crowded with all kinds of musical activity as the young composer-to-be continued to study and teach simultaneously, finally deciding to dedicate his life to the service of God and the Church through the ministry of music. It was his good fortune to study for a while under D. A. Towner (1850-1919), composer of "Trust And Obey", who instructed him in conducting and hymn singing in Chicago, where Towner was on the faculty of the "Windy City's" famed Moody Bible Institute. Later Charles H. Gabriel, whose "Awakening Chorus" is a perennial choral favorite, taught Huston the fundamentals of composition, especially as it related to the writing of hymn tunes. It was not until his twenty-seventh year that Frank produced his first successful gospel song, "We shall gather 'round the throne", but that proved to be an auspicious beginning. The encouragement he received from the response of many congregations to his initial effort was all young Huston needed to set him on the creative road he was to follow for more than six succeeding decades.

It was in April of 1909, while Frank was directing the music for Evangelist W. S. Buchanan in a series of services being held in Providence Christian Church, Scranton Pennsylvania, that he was inspired to write the music of "It Pays To Serve Jesus", one of his finest gospel hymns. His hosts during the Scranton engagement were Mr. and Mrs. Gwylym Edwards, choir director and Church organist respectively of the Providence congregation, in whose home Huston was entertained. One day while Frank was musing at the keyboard of the Edwards' piano, a melody suddenly came to him which he decided was worth saving. So he quickly wrote it down on a piece of music paper which he usually carried around in his pocket for just such emergencies, and promptly forgot all about it.

Returning to his home in Indianapolis after the Pennsylvania meeting for a period of rest and fellowship with his family, he brought his new tune with him. A few days later he paid a visit to an eighty-two year old friend, M. E. Mick, a devout member of the Meridian Street Methodist Church of that city. During their conversation, Mick suddenly said to Huston, "Brother Huston, you have written so many good songs, won't you write one for me on the subject we have just been discussing, and call it 'It Pays to Serve Jesus'?" Frank interrupted to remind his aged friend that there was already a published song bearing that title, whereupon Mick replied, "I know there is, but I think you can write a better one. Won't you promise to try?" Huston agreed, because of his close friendship with the older man, but didn't actually make a special effort to comply with the request until some time later, during another evangelistic series being held in Harrisburg, Pennsylvania.

While a guest in the Hartzog home in that city, Huston recalled Mick's plea of several weeks earlier, so he went to the fine piano in the living room of his host and hostess with the hope that he would be able to come up with something that would satisfy his elderly friend back home. Suddenly he recalled the manuscript in his pocket, and, out of sheer curiosity, he took it out, placed it on the music rack of the piano and played through it. Intrigued with what he had composed and then completely forgotten, he played it a second time and then a third, while the words of a stanza and chorus fell into place almost spontaneously. Before he knew it, he was singing a brand new hymn to his own original tune,

"The service of Jesus true pleasure affords, In Him there is joy
    without an alloy;
'Tis heaven to trust Him and rest on His words; It pays to serve
    Jesus each day."

Soon the second and third stanzas followed, and within fifteen
minutes, the new song was finished. The composer sang it that
very night as a sacred solo, although he had written it as a duet.
When it was published sometime later, while Huston was engaged
in a meeting in Halifax, Nova Scotia, its popularity was assured,
and, in the intervening decades, not a note or a word has been
changed. Copyrighted the very same year, 1909, it rapidly spread
throughout the Churches and Sunday Schools of the composer's
own denomination, The Disciples of Christ, and was soon adopted
by The Christian Endeavor societies as an "official" hymn. Since
that time, it has been translated into a number of other languages,
and, when the composer renewed his copyright in 1937, the song
was continuing to grow in popularity and usefulness. Speaking
of this familiar gospel song, Huston himself said, "The writer
never considered this song as a masterpiece, either from a literary
or musical viewpoint, but he is thoroughly convinced that it
carries one of the most vital truths to be found anywhere today,
a truth which, if only believed and applied, would solve more
problems of real life than the councils of men have solved in the
last century."

After ninteen successful years as a "singing evangelist", Frank
Huston was ordained to the ministry of his Church in Indianapolis in 1915. His musical ministry led him in 187 evangelistic
campaigns with forty-four different preachers all over the United
States, while, during the more than twenty-six years of his preaching ministry, he served eight Churches, two of which assumed the
full-time support of a pastor as a result of his labors. His contribution to American Church music was recognized when he was
voted membership in ASCAP (American Society of Composers,
Authors and Publishers). At this writing, in 1958, Frank Huston
is a resident of the Florida Christian Home in Jacksonville, Florida, from which "home base" he continues to spread the gospel
of hope and Christian cheer through his wonderful gift of song,
while the gospel hymns and songs he was privileged to write dur-

ing his long and active life continue to make his influence felt in the far corners of Christendom. In his second-best-known gospel song "The Christ of the Cross", Huston wrote two of the finest lines he ever penned, lines in which he confessed his own Christion faith in these words,

"For though we must cherish the old rugged cross, 'Tis only the Christ can redeem."

That he glorified His Lord in his music, and that he fittingly sang the praise of Christ in his hymns and gospel songs, is the unanimous testimony of those believers whose lives have been enriched by the preacher-poet, Frank C. Huston, whose personal Christian life mirrored the words of the Chorus of his finest hymn:

It pays to serve Jesus, it pays every day; It pays every step of the way;
Though the pathway to glory may sometimes be drear, You'll be happy each step of the way.

17.

IVORY PALACES

The gospel hymn familiarly known as "Ivory Palaces" is just about as Presbyterian a sacred song as there is, not because of its theological content but because of the denominational affiliation of the men who were instrumental in creating it. The inspiration back of the writing of the words and music of this perennial favorite was none other than the distinguished Presbyterian preacher, author, evangelist and world-traveller, Rev. Dr. John Wilbur Chapman (1859-1918). This Indiana born native American, after studying at Oberlin College and Lake Forest University, from which he was graduated in 1879, entered Lane Theological Seminary, receiving his degree from that post-graduate institution for the training of preachers three years later, in 1882. Following his ordination to the Presbyterian ministry that very same year, he served several Churches of his denomination in Albany, Philadelphia and New York City, finally relinquishing the pastorate and becoming a full-time evangelist.

The success which attended his evangelistic labors in America brought him invitations to preach in some of the leading pulpits of Great Britain and thus it came to pass that while preaching in England in 1914, he made the acquaintance of a twenty-three year old pianist by the name of Henry Barraclough. The gifted musician, a native of Windhill, Yorkshire, England, where he had been born on December 14, 1891, had received his education in the schools of Bradford, England, and, following the completion of his academic studies, had held such varied positions as an insurance company claims adjuster, and private secretary to a member of Parliament. In January 1914, he joined the Chapman-Alexander evangelistic team, made up of Dr. J. Wilbur Chapman, preacher and Mr. Charles M. Alexander, song-leader. For the next three years, Barraclough played the piano while Alexander sang and Chapman preached.

When the first world war broke out in Europe in the summer of 1914, the three men left the British Isles for the United States and held meetings in several southern cities. In the summer of the following year, 1915, they were invited to visit a rapidly developing Presbyterian summer Assembly center located a few miles from Black Moutain in the hills of western North Carolina, known as Montreat (a contraction of "The Mountain Retreat Association"). By that time, Barraclough had heard all of Dr. Chapman's best sermons, and knew those which the thrice-wed evangelist delivered to small groups and those he perferred to preach to larger congregations. One of the minister's personal favorites, which he normally preached only to small, intimate groups of professing Christians, was an unusual sermon based upon an unusual text found in Psalm 45:8, "All thy garments smell of myrrh and aloes and cassia, out of the ivory palaces, whereby they have made thee glad". Many who were attending the Montreat gatherings that particular summer had heard of that particular message, and when they learned that Dr. Chapman was to deliver several sermons during the summer series, they urged him to include the one on "Ivory Palaces".

Chapman was loathe to give in to their requests, but finally agreed to comply. The congregation that greeted him that memorable night included more than two-thousand people. Although Barraclough and Alexander had already heard the talk a dozen or more times they listened with growing interest as Chapman developed his sermon, using the outline that was now so familiar to them. The inspiration of the tremendous congregation was not lost on the preacher, for he delivered his address with more intense fervor than ever before, until even the song-leader and pianist felt the inspiration of the hour. Chapman spoke of the "myrrh, whose fragrance fills our beings with joy" and the "aloes, which symbolized our Lord's sorrow" as well as the "cassia, with healing in its touch", preaching with such eloquence that the twenty-four year old musician saw in his exposition something he had never seen before.

After the crowds had dispersed at the close of the meeting, Mr. Alexander invited some friends to drive with him to the YMCA summer conference grounds, located a few miles from Montreat on the slope of the mountain on the far side of the valley, at Blue Ridge, North Carolina. Barraclough went along, sitting in the front seat with the driver. As the others visited, the young pianist began thinking about the sermon and the possibilities he had seen in it which had escaped him heretofore, and, before he knew it, the words and music of a chorus based upon Chapman's message came crowding into his mind, a chorus which pictured Christ as coming out of the ivory palaces, moved by his great, eternal love to save a world of sin and woe. Picking up the outline of the sermon, he soon fashioned three stanzas to match the spirit and mood of the refrain. When the party stopped for a few moments at a village store enroute to Blue Ridge, Henry hastily jotted down his three stanzas and chorus on the back of a visiting card, which, he later confessed, was "the only piece of writing material" he could lay his hands on at the time. The author denied that he wrote down his lines on the cuff of his white shirt, as was told by some in later years who professed to know the truth about the writing of "Ivory Palaces".

When he returned to his hotel room at Montreat that night, he wrote out the words and music of his new gospel song, adding the fourth and final stanza a short while later after a conference with Dr. Chapman.

The next morning Mrs. Alexander and Mr. Albert Brown, the baritone soloist with the evangelistic party, introduced "Ivory Palaces" to a Montreat congregation as a result of which initial rendition, it was applauded and accepted and found its way into the hymals and gospel song books of Christendom.

Dr. Chapman was honored by his denomination in being elected to her highest office, that of Moderator of the General Assembly of the (northern, or USA) Presbyterian Church. A tireless worker, he suffered thirteen breakdowns in health and wrote at least fourteen books before his death three years after inspiring Barraclough to write his most famous gospel song, passing away at the age of fify-nine in 1918.

The author-composer served with the A.E.F. in France during the first world war, returning home to his adopted America to become closely affiliated with Dr. Chapman's Church, the Presbyterian Church in the USA. He rapidly advanced from committee secretary to Manager of the Office of the General Assembly, and then, for thirty years, from 1923 to 1953, as Dr. Henry Barraclough, having received an honorary Doctor of Laws degree from Bloomfield College and Seminary in New Jersey, he filled the position of Manager of the Assembly's Department of Administration. In 1953 he was elected one of the two Associate Stated Clerks of his Church, an office he continued to fill when the United Presbyterian Church in the U.S.A. was created in May, 1958. On the local level, he has been active in many capacities in the Tioga Presbyterian Church of Philadelphia from 1922 to the present time. Married, but childless, he continues to render faithful service to the cause of Christ and His Kingdom, and it was through his personal courtesy that the facts contained in this story came to my attention.

The sermon he made into a song when he was twenty-four, copyrighted in 1915 by Charles M. Alexander, has sung its way around the world, and will undoubtedly continue to be used of God long after its creator has left the Church militant to become a member of the Church triumphant!

18.

JESUS LOVES ME, THIS I KNOW

Anna Bartlett Warner was thirty-six years old when she and her older sister, Susan, collaborated on another novel. Quite a few years had passed since their first best-seller had come from the publisher's press, but following that initial success, the two sisters had become as avid writers as they had been readers in their early teens. It was not unusual to find several new Warner books on the shelves of the book stores, together with copies of the perennially popular volumes they had been turning out now for nearly a decade since "The Wide, Wide World" had become an overnight sensation in 1850, Susan's thirty-first year.

Inspired by their sudden success, the sisters thought nothing of turning out two or three new books a year, all of which were widely purchased and eagerly read.

It was in 1859 that the Warners, still publishing their books under their pen names "Elizabeth Wetherell" (Susan) and "Amy Lothrop" (Anna), finished their latest novel, "Say and Seal". It was such a long work that the publisher brought it out in two volumes of more than five-hundred pages each. The demand for the novel become so great that in 1860 the sisters, confessing their joint authorship in the preface, authorized a one-volume edition to be prepared, a business venture that proved to be a highly successful one both for the authors and the publishers.

Although the Putnam Publishing Company had had to be pushed by George Putnam's mother into accepting "The Wide Wide World", the publisher later admitted that it was one of the wisest decisions his company ever made.

Now there was no question of finding a publisher. It was rather a question of furnishing him all the material he wanted as rapidly as they could prepare it. Little dreaming that they were soon to enshrine their names forever upon the hearts and minds of

Christian children the world over, Susan and Anna wove a simple plot around a sweet girl named Faith Derrick, a faithful Sunday School teacher who was quite obviously in love with her, John Endecott Linden, and a sick little boy who died before the end of Volume II, Johnny Fax. Whether the names Faith and Fax (facts) were contrived or merely coincidental the authors refused to reveal.

On page 115 of the 1860 one-volume, one-thousand page edition of this novel, the authors tell of Johnny's heart-tugging sickness, and the tender loving care lavished upon him by Faith and Mr. Linden. In Volume I they had written of a brighter and happier day when the three of them had accompanied a Sunday School class of boys on a picnic in the nearby woods, where, with Johnny sitting quietly on his lap, Mr. Linden had joined some of the boys in singing an original hymn "I want to be an angel".

Now, some time later, and several hundreds of pages further on, little Johnny lies critically sick, and, despite all that Faith and Mr. Linden can do, seems destined for death. When Mr. Linden asks the lad what he can do for him, Johnny holds up his tiny arms to his Sunday School teacher and says, "Walk — like last night". Then, picking up the feverish lad, Mr. Linden slowly walks back and forth across the room, the motion of his walking having an immediate soothing and quieting effect upon the boy.

As he became quieter, and as Faith stood to one side looking on in silence, Johnny said, "Sing". Mr. Linden, continuing to walk back and forth, rocking the child in his arms, began to sing a brand new song, one that Johnny had never heard before, but one which was to endear Susan and Anna Warner to children the world over from that moment on. As Faith listened, she heard every word clearly and distinctly, for Mr. Linden was singing softly:

Jesus loves me, this I know, For the Bible tells me so;
Little ones to him belong, They are weak but he is strong.

Jesus loves me — he who died Heaven's gate to open wide;
He will wash away my sin, Let his little child come in.

Jesus loves me, loves me still, Though I'm very weak and ill;
From his shining throne on high Comes to watch me where I lie.

Jesus loves me — he will stay Close beside me all the way,
Then his little child will take Up to heaven for his dear sake.

A few hours later, just after Mr. Linden had read some of
Johnny's favorite verses about the beauty and glory of God's
heavenly kingdom from the Book of Revelation, and they had
spoken together about "the city that hath foundations", God
called the soul of little Johnny Fax back to himself after Mr.
Linden had said softly, "We were permitted to show him the way
at first, Faith, but he is showing it to us now".

The very next year, 1861, the well-known composer of many
popular hymn tunes and gospel song tunes, William B. Bradbury
(1818-1868) discovered this poetic gem and immediately set it
to music, adding, in the custom of the day, an original "Chorus"
all his very own: Yes, Jesus loves me; Yes, Jesus loves me:
Yes, Jesus loves me; The Bible tells me so.

From their home on Constitution Island, near West Point,
New York, the talented daughters of a New York lawyer, Henry
W. Warner, Esquire, turned out book after book and volume
after volume. In addition, they conducted Sunday School classes
for cadets from the West Point Military Academy, their interest
in that school dating from the days when their father's brother,
Thomas, had served as West Point's Chaplain as well as Professor
of Geography, History and Ethics.

The family sitting room in which these weekly classes were
held, with its little organ on which Susan and Anna would accompany the hymns the group sang, and a copy of Stuart's
famous painting of George Washington hanging over the fire-
place, is preserved today just as it was many, many years ago,
while the Warner home, "Wood Crag", has become something
of a shrine, visited by hundreds of people anually.

Bought by Mr. Warner in 1836, it became the home in which
he and his two daughters lived with his sister, Fanny, as their
house-keeper, following Mrs. Warner's death and the loss of their
Long Island home in the financial panic of 1837. It was the wish
of Susan and Anna Warner, that, at their death Constitution
Island be turned over to the United States to become a permanent part of the United States Military Academy, at West Point.
Although Susan passed away in 1885, Anna lived until 1915,

making final arrangements for the transfer of this valuable, historic and strategic piece of property during the first decade of the twentieth century, a gift that inspired a personal letter of thanks from President Theodore Roosevelt.

Today, Martelaer's Rock (Constitution Island's original name, supposedly given it by some Dutch settlers who named the island "Martyr's Cliff") has become a national shrine, and a grateful nation continues to pay its tributes to the Warner sisters for their thoughtful and generous gift as tourists come from far and wide to pay their personal tributes and homage to their memory.

But few of them know that these same talented women gave to the Christian world several of her loveliest songs for children, among them, "I want to be an angel", "Jesus loves me, this I know" and "Jesus bids us shine with a clear pure light". If they had done only that, they would have enriched the world to a marvelous extent during their busy and fruitful lives.

19.

JEWELS

"Little children may be diamonds in the rough, but they are jewels just the same," William Orcutt Cushing said to a co-worker in the Massachusetts Sunday School where they both served as teachers. "Sometimes I lose patience with them, it's true, but then I remember the words of the Lord Jesus when he said 'If ye then being evil know how to give good gifts to your children, how much more will your father in heaven give good things to them that ask him?' (Matthew 7:11). And when I recall how good God has been to me in spite of my badness to Him, I become a bit more understanding and patient with the little children who come under my supervision and care Sunday after Sunday."

His fellow teacher smiled and said, "You're right, William. We must always treat the children who are consigned to us with the same spirit which characterizes God's treatment of each one of us, adult, youth, or child. In fact, the Psalmist said a great deal when he wrote, 'Like as a father pitieth his children, so the Lord pitieth them that fear him. For he knoweth our frame; he remembereth that we are dust' (Psalm 103: 13-14). When we deal with our little charges as God deals with us, when we remember and pity them as he remembers and pities us, that makes a difference, doesn't it?"

Thirty-three year old Rev. W. O. Cushing (1823-1902) nodded his head in agreement. "It does," he said. "It makes a great deal of difference."

Cushing had little sympathy with some of the conservative adults who looked with scorn upon the whole Sunday School movement as a waste of time and energy. "If some understanding older people had taken more time with some of those old fogies when they were little, they wouldn't have turned out the way they did," he said, a sentiment with which many of his fellow teachers and Sunday School workers heartily concurred.

The fact that he had been converted as a child colored Cushing's theology to the extent that he felt moved to present the Gospel in all its power to every child within his reach, in order that each one could experience the change that had come to him so unexpectedly and so early in life. "Jesus said over and over that unless we become like little children, we cannot inherit the kingdom of heaven," preacher-poet Cushing often said from his pulpit. "And becoming like a little child means that we do not try to reason out God by the powers of intellect alone, but we accept Him as children trust their earthly parents. Children believe that their parents are who they say they are, so Christians believe that Jesus was who He claimed He was, and that God was all that Jesus said He was. Jesus never debated or argued the existence of God; He merely accepted it, and lived His days in the light of its reality. In that way, He became as a little child and thereby inherited the kingdom of heaven. While logic can never warm a child's heart as much as love, so logic about the things of the kingdom of God often leaves us cold, while love warms us up and makes life worth living," the pastor concluded.

He received little children because his Master had said "Who-ever shall receive one such little child in my name, receiveth me" and he shewed mercy to them in the name of Him who commend-ed those who gave a cup of cold water to one of these little ones, and thereby did it unto him. Carefully advising those who stood in the way of dedicated men and women who laboured faithfully and diligently in the Sunday School movement, he warned the opponents by means of the words of the Lord Himself, who said "Whoso shall offend one of these little ones, believe me, it were better for him that a millstone were hanged about his neck and that he were drowned in the depth of the sea." (Matthew 18:6).

"The children should always be 'suffered' or 'permitted' to come unto the Master," he stated forcefully, "for of such is the kingdom of heaven. If they are let alone, they will naturally gravitate to him, for he attracts them by the magnetic power of his personality, and by the radiant and warm love which glows from his countenance."

When Cushing found the words recorded in Malachi 3:17, everything in his heart that loved little children came into sharp focus and inspired him to write the song which was to sing its way around the world. The words he read were, "And they shall be mine, saith the Lord, in that day when I make up my jewels."

For the children in his own Sunday School, William O. Cushing wrote his new song, entitled "Jewels," that memorable day in 1856, and soon they were ringing the rafters as they sang:

When he cometh, when he cometh To make up his jewels;
All his jewels, precious jewels, His loved and his own;
Like the stars of the morning, His bright crown adorning,
They shall shine in their beauty, Bright gems for his crown.

It only remained for the composer of the most popular songs of the Civil War era, George Frederick Root (1820-1895) to write his lilting music, and the song was well on its way to immortality.

This was not the only song on which Cushing and Root collaborated. Some years later, Root wrote a tune for a popular song, which was entitled "The Little Octoroon". He sent the music to his preacher friend with the request that he try to do a bit better for it than the poem for which he had composed the music. Cushing hummed the music over and over all day, trying to find just the words that would enable him to use the music in his Sunday School work. When he heard someone speaking of the bells of heaven ringing over the return of a ransomed sinner, he knew he had what he had been looking for, and in a very short while, he wrote the stanzas for his popular gospel song "Ring the bells of heaven" which was perfectly adapted to Root's stirring tune.

Root himself became the most famous composer of his day, because, from his facile fingers came such well-known war songs as "Tramp, tramp, tramp, the boys are marching", "The battle cry of freedom", "Just before the battle, mother", and the heartbreaking "The vacant chair". In addition, he continued to write for Church and Sunday School use, and today his hymn tunes "Varina" (There is a land of pure delight) and "Ellon" (The wise may bring their learning) are widely used, while his songs, "Why do you wait, dear brother?" and "The hem of his garment" are still included in collections of gospel songs in many parts of the country.

Glee clubs in many men's colleges still sing Root's well-known song "There's music in the air" while his music that set many men's feet marching into battle in 1861-1865, "Tramp, tramp, tramp", has been adapted to the stanzas of Rev. Dr. C. H. Woolston, "Jesus loves the little children, All the children of the world." And in God's sight they are still the jewels that Cushing considered them and worth more than all the gold in all the world.

20

LIFE IS LIKE A MOUNTAIN RAILROAD

When the long-awaited dream of a practical steam engine finally became reality, one half-educated clergyman felt that the new invention was a defiance of the laws of God. In order to bolster his own convictions in that regard, as well as to attempt to persuade his congregation that there were sound Scriptural foundations for his peculiar beliefs, he delivered a sermon against railroads, taking as his text the familiar words of the marriage vows, "What God hath joined together, let no man put asunder" (Matthew 19:6).

In his unusual pulpit tirade he said, "If it is true that we are not to put asunder what God has joined together, it is also true that we are not to put together what God has put asunder. And God put water and fire asunder, and any attempt to bring them together in order to make the steam that is necessary to make an engine run is a direct violation of the law of God."

Fortunately for posterity, his message had no effect whatsoever on the future of railroading. Many years later, another minister was so intrigued and fascinated by everything connected with steam engines and trains and railroads that he saw nearly everything through a railroader's eyes and spoke of events in a trainman's figure of speech.

The author of the New Testament book of James had written, in answer to the query, "What is your life?" this reply, "For ye are a vapor that appeareth for a little time and then vanisheth away" (James 4:14). But the Rev. M. E. Abbey, a Baptist clergyman of Atlanta, Georgia in the last decade of the nineteenth century, pictured life in terms which the Biblical author would not have understood, drawing a striking parallel between railroading as he had experienced it in his younger days and every day living as he had participated in it for almost three-quarters of a century. Putting his feelings in poetic form, the aging minister wrote several stanzas, the first of which contained these picturesque lines:

"Life is like a mountain railroad, With an engineer that's brave;
We must make the run successful From the cradle to the grave;
Watch the curves, the fills, the tunnels; Never falter, never quail;
Keep your hand upon the throttle, and your eye upon the rail.

His chorus went as follows:

Blessed Saviour, thou wilt guide us, Till we reach that blissful shore,
Where the angels wait to join us In thy praise forevermore."

Subsequent stanzas mentioned "grades of trial" and the "bridge of strife", which Christians could surmount only if they made Christ their conductor "on this lightning train of life", while he spoke of heaven as the "Union Depot" where the great Superintendent waited to welcome the weary pilgrims home.

Abbey didn't know exactly what to do with his verses until he ran into Rev. Charles D. Tillman, a fellow Georgian, on the streets of Atlanta a few days later. Rushing up to greet him, Abbey pressed a piece of paper into Tillman's hand, saying "Charlie, I have written a railroad poem and I want you to take it and see if you can set it to music."

Although he had had very little formal musical training, composing music was no chore for the Alabama-born Methodist preacher. In 1887, at the age of twenty-six, he had had the audacity to publish his first book, a little thirty-two page collection of gospel songs, entitled "Little Light." The success of this initial effort so encouraged the self-taught singer, pianist and composer, that he was to publish twenty more volumes in the years that lay ahead.

Born in the Alabama town of Tallassee, a typical southern factory village, on March 20, 1861, in the home of a Methodist evangelist, Charlie Tillman grew up to love everything that pertained to the Church, especially her rich heritage of music. Even though he was his preacher-father's constant companion for many a special series of revival and evangelistic services during his early years, Charlie always looked back upon an evening in August, 1886 as the time when he "personally found the Lord" in a meeting being held in Cuba Station, Alabama.

In his late teens and early twenties he managed to combine house-painting with the study of music, drawing a music staff on the side of a house, and mastering it while pushing his brush up and down on either side of the notes. Commenting on this original practice, Tillman said later, "I would paint up to it, study it, move it further up, paint up to it again, study it some more, and so on. In this way I learned to read music. Afterward I began writing out melodies."

For the next few years he was a travelling salesman, the young composer-to-be boasting of the fact that he made it a rule to entertain his prospective customers musically before attempting to sell them some of his wares. In fact he swapped songs for food and lodging on several occasions when his income failed to match his outgo! But when he finally established himself, he made Christmas Eve of 1889 the most memorable day of the year, taking Miss Anna Killingsworth, a native of Augusta, Georgia, as his bride the day before the Christmas of his twenty-seventh year. To this union one son and four daughters were born. The boy died in 1910 at the age of fifteen, while the four daughters lived to enjoy their parents Golden Wedding Anniversary on Christmas Eve, 1939.

Charlie read over Abbey's verses and quickly realized that a successful tune for those lines had to be extremely simple and yet melodic enough to be singable. With that in mind, he hurried to his room, put the piece of paper on the music rack of the organ, sat down at the keyboard, pumped up the bellows and began to sing.

Almost as spontaneously as the Baptist clergyman had written his stanzas, the Methodist minister fashioned his original tune, a piece of music as unostentatious as the words to which it was so soon to be wedded. Using the same basic chords around which Ira D. Sankey had composed his tune for "The ninety and nine", Charlie Tillman completed his arrangement, but its very simplicity caused him to hesitate before submitting it to a publisher. In fact he even sought out some musical friends, and had them try their hands at composing a tune for Abbey's lines, but when none of the other settings satisfied him, he figured his was a mite better than theirs and was finally persuaded to send it in.

Almost before the ink was dry on the first printing, the railroad men of the country had taken the song to their hearts and made it their very own. The composer said, "I am giving God all the glory for my little success". He became known as "one of the greatest song leaders of the southern Methodist Church" as well as "an eminently successful evangelist", preaching hundreds of sermons and composing thousands of gospel song tunes, many of which became popular during his own lifetime.

Teaming up with the evangelist Sam Jones, Tillman travelled throughout the southern states, singing for the glory of God, his own "infectious sense of humor" being sharpened by his close fellowship with this remarkable preacher-humorist of the turn of the century. In 1935, Tillman made a sound movie, playing and singing many of his well-known hymns, spirituals and gospel songs, since it was his conviction that "the talking screen can be made as powerful a factor for teaching right living as the pulpit".

When he died in Atlanta in 1943 at the age of eighty-two, he was one of the city's most prominent and best beloved citizens. Although some classical critics may "look down their noses" at Tillman's tunes, no one can deny that they, in their way, were used of God to bless and to inspire several generations of believers, and "Life is like a mountain railroad" will continue to be popular as long as railroading exists and as long as brave engineers seek to follow the example of Christ, heeding the admonition of Abbey and Tillman,

"Always mindful of obstruction, Do your duty, never fail;
Keep your hand upon the throttle, and your eye upon the rail."

21

MY MOTHER'S BIBLE

Among the noblest hymns on the Bible in the English language are Bishop W. W. How's majestic "O word of God incarnate", William Cowper's "A glory gilds the sacred page", Miss Anne Steele's "Father of mercies, in thy word", Rev. Washington Gladden's "Behold a sower from afar", Hugh Stowell's "Lord of all power and might" and Mary A. Lathbury's Chatauqua hymn "Break thou the bread of life".

Undoubtedly the subject will continue to intrigue hymn writers for centuries to come, and hymns more stately than those produced during the last century may come from the pens of poets yet unborn. In fact, this columnist was inspired to write a hymn on this subject during a rather lengthy and boring debate that consumed several valuable hours of time at a session of the Virginia Annual Conference of the Methodist Church, held in the Main Street Methodist Church, Danville, Va., in June of 1939. Weary of hearing the brethren pontificate on a wide variety of unrelated topics, I browsed through the hymnal, only to be struck with the dearth of hymns on The Holy Scriptures. In a few moments, on the back of an envelope, I had written two stanzas to be sung to the familiar strains of Hans Leo Hassler's hymn tune "Passion Chorale" (O sacred head now wounded), containing these lines:

O Book divine and holy, enriched with ancient lore,
Bestowed for man's redemption from God's unfailing store;
Within thy sacred pages, we trace man's age-long quest
For peace surpassing knowledge, for solace, strength and rest.

O Book inspired, inspiring, revealing in thy span
The unveiled souls of mortals, the father's wondrous plan;
While following in thy gospels, the footsteps of our Lord,
We strive to be more Christlike, and build a world for God.

While a hymn may be defined as "a religious poem addressed to or descriptive of one of the members of the Holy Trinity, the Father, the Son, or the Holy Ghost", a gospel song may be as accurately described as "a religious poem that is descriptive of one's own individual Christian experience".

The hymn is objective while the song is subjective, and of all the gospel songs based upon the Holy Bible, none is more familiar or better loved than "My Mother's Bible". Written in the sentimental style that characterized many sacred and popular songs of the closing decades of the last century, it possesses that "tear-jerking" quality which endears it to some people while others regard it from the seats of the scornful as unworthy of a place in a Christian hymnal. Nevertheless there was a time not too many years ago when evangelistic singers could "bring down the house" by singing:

"There's a dear and precious Book, though it's worn and faded now,
Which recalls the happy days of long ago;
When I stood at Mother's knee, with her hand upon my brow,
And I heard her voice in gentle tones and low.

Chorus: Blessed book, precious book,
On thy tear-stained leaves I love to look;
Thou art sweeter day by day, As I walk the narrow way
That leads at last to that bright home above."

It was in 1893, the year that Rev. Charlie D. Tillman was called upon to substitute for the great Ira D. Sankey as song-leader for a World Convention of Christian Workers which attracted six thousand delegates to Boston, that the Alabama-born Methodist evangelist and singer was working with Rev. M. B. Williams in a series of revival services in New York State.

One day, as he was looking through the available hymnals and songbooks for an appropriate song with which to conclude a sermon on The Holy Bible, Evangelist Williams said to his co-worker, Singer Tillman, "Charlie, I want a Bible song."

Tillman, a self-taught musician who had published his first book of gospel songs, a thirty-two page collection entitled "Little

Light" only six years earlier, replied, "M.B., you write the words and I will see what I can do for the music."

Accepting the challenge in the spirit in which it had been offered, Williams picked up a Bible which his Mother had given to him after she had used it faithfully for many years, opened it until he found a blank page near the cover, reached in his pocket for a pencil, and, with the sentiments and memories of childhood creeping through the years, began to write down the stanzas of "My Mother's Bible". Within fifteen minutes his work was done, and he read to his song-leader the three stanzas and chorus of the new gospel song. Charlie was deeply moved by the personal witness contained in the lines, especially those of the second stanza, which read:

"There she read of Jesus' love, as he blest the children dear,
How he suffered, bled and died upon the tree;
Of his heavy load of care; then she dried my flowing tear
With her kisses, as she said it was for me."

As Williams read the lines, Charlie picked out an appropriate melody, and when M. B. looked up as he finished reading, Tillman said, "M. B., that's fine".

The preacher smiled as he extended his hand and remarked, "Give me your hand. That is the first thing I ever did that you said was any good."

Some weeks later, Tillman wrote down his new musical setting, a tune based upon the same simple harmonies that characterized his popular success, "Life's Railway To Heaven" and from that day to this, not a single note of his melody and harmony has been altered.

Tillman, who made his home in Atlanta, Georgia for many years, became widely known and loved as one of southern Methodism's finest evangelists and singers, composing thousands of gospel song tunes during his long and eventful life of eighty-two years. A native of Tallassee, Alabama, where he was born on March 20, 1861, "converted" in Cuba Station, Alabama in August, 1886, married to Miss Anna Killingsworth of Augusta, Georgia, on Christmas Eve, 1889, Charlie and Anna lived to celebrate their Golden Wedding anniversary in 1939, an occasion made brighter by the presence of their four daughters, their only son having passed away in 1910 at the age of fifteen.

Through the kindness and courtesy of one of the Tillman daughters, Mrs. Jewel Tillman Burns of Atlanta, this columnist was able to learn the details of the life and musical ministry of this remarkable man of God, who early dedicated his talents to the service of the King of Kings, and laboured lovingly and loyally to develop the gifts with which his heavenly Father had endowed him.

As long as Christians sing "Life is like a mountain railroad", "My Mother's Bible", and "The old time religion", the expanding influence of this one life will continue to spread and the inspiration of these songs will continue to be a blessing.

Before his death in 1943, Charlie had published twenty collections of gospel songs in addition to several other volumes, including a "Day School Singer", "The Assembly Book" which was adopted by the public schools of his adopted state of Georgia. But his deepest sense of satisfaction must have come from the knowledge that some of his compositions were accepted by the Churches and became a permanent part of their heritage of hymns and gospel songs.

22.

NEAR TO THE HEART OF GOD

Westminster College in Fulton, Missouri, is famous because it was on the campus of that school that Sir Winston Churchill delivered his "Iron Curtain" address on March 5, 1946. However, Westminster is not the only well-known or world-renowned Missouri College. She must share her honors with Park College in Parkville, Missouri, since that school will long be remembered and loved as the scene of the writing of one of Christendom's loveliest gospel hymns, and the site of its initial rendition.

The McAfee family has long been identified with the Presbyterian Church and Park College, and the fortunes of the two have been intricately intertwined for several generations. The elder statesman of the long line of McAfees was John Armstrong McAfee, one of the original founders as well as the first president of the Missouri Church college. The six distinguished children of the first administrator and his wife were brought up in the atmosphere of Christian education and culture and it was perfectly natural that their own lives would figure in the life and labors of the institution their father helped to establish.

So it came to pass that in the decade just prior to the birth of the twentieth century, five McAfee sons, Lowell, Howard, Lapsley, Cleland and Ernest, and one McAfee daughter, Helen, were residents of Parkville. One of the boys, Cleland, who was destined in later and more mature years to receive the highest honors of his denomination in being elevated to the position of Moderator of the General Assembly of the Presbyterian Church (the northern branch of the still-divided Presbyterian communion) was serving not only as college pastor, but also as choir director of the college church.

In addition to these heavy responsibilities he filled the faculty chair of Philosophy and, when he was not preaching, lecturing, singing or counselling, he assumed oversight of various other educational and religious activities connected with student and church life. From morning prayers at 6 A. M. each day until midnight nearly every night, he was hard at work in the many and varied encounters which make life on a college campus far from dull. His powers of intellect were early evident, for he graduated from Park in 1884, a youth of eighteen, and it was after the completion of his graduate studies at New York's well-known Union Theological Seminary that he returned to his Alma Mater in the capacities of pastor, professor, preacher, performer, pedagogue and presbyter, tasks big enough to frighten a lesser man out of his wits.

To balance all of this, and to give his own life the enrichment which only a happy Christian home can insure, Cleland married Hattie Brown, a talented girl who had matriculated in Park College the fall following his graduation, receiving her diploma four years later, in the early summer of 1888.

To keep himself constantly creative, pastor McAfee began to prepare an original hymn for the choir of his Church to sing each quarter when the Sacrament of the Holy Communion was administered to his growing congregation. He would usually write his stanzas on the same theme he chose for his brief sermon, setting them to appropriate music as soon as the muse created the proper mood. His people began to anticipate their gifted minister's hymns and tunes with the same eagerness with which they looked forward to his sermons.

Then it was that tragedy struck with unexplained suddenness, leaving in its wake unmerited sorrow and undeserved heartache. Diphtheria, that dreaded disease, caught Howard and Lucy McAfee's two precious daughters in its deadly clutches and claimed them as its victims.

The brothers and sister with their close-knit families offered to the bereaved parents all the love and understanding and sympathy their hearts could muster but no one dared try to explain the reason for loss of the two little girls, or attempt to understand the mysterious workings of a supposedly beneficent providence. Cleland was as distressed as Howard and as much at a loss as to know "Why" as his devoted brother. While he felt he could not peer into the mind of his Heavenly Father to understand "all mysteries and all knowledge", he did feel, with a certainty that could neither be mocked nor destroyed, that, through Jesus, he could gaze into the heart of the Almighty and know that God was love, infinite, eternal and unchangeable love.

Although there were many things about the passing of his two nieces that he failed to comprehend, Cleland never doubted in his heart that God was still his Father, and his Father was still all-loving and all-love. With those thoughts burning in his own heart, the young pastor began to think about the communion hymn he wanted to write for the following Sunday morning, and soon he was saying to himself "We can find peace and comfort if we stay near to the heart of God". Soon the words were flowing from his facile pen, and he found himself writing,

"There is a place of quiet rest, Near to the heart of God;
A place where sin cannot molest, Near to the heart of God."

Near to God's heart was "comfort sweet" and "full release" he continued, until he finished his third and last stanza, adding in the chorus the prayer that Jesus, our Blest Redeemer, would "hold us, who wait before Thee", "Near to the heart of God."

His tune was as simple, sincere, spiritual and singable as his stanzas, and when his choir members sang it from the composer's manuscript at their scheduled Saturday night rehearsal a few days later, they were so deeply moved that they went in a body to Howard's home and sang the new hymn "outside the darkened, quarantined house." The next morning they sang it again as Cleland's communion hymn and then proceeded to forget all about it, as the sting of the sorrow which inspired it gradually died away and was almost forgotten.

But another brother, Lapsley, refused to set the hymn aside, and when he became pastor of the First Presbyterian Church in Berkeley, California, he taught it to his choir and congregation, and soon other believers were being comforted with its note of quiet assurance and seeking surcease from their own sorrows by getting closer and nearer to the heart of God.

It was not until 1903 that the Lorenz Publishing Company secured a copyright for the words and music, one they proudly renewed twenty-eight years later, in 1931, after the hymn had spread its message of hope to the far corners of the Christian world and been accepted as worthy of inclusion in the hymnals not only of the Presbyterian Church but of sister denominations as well.

Although Cleland Boyd McAfee (1866-1944) earned well deserved honors as a Professor at McCormick Theological Seminary, Chicago, a pastor of several large Presbyterian Churches, a writer and editor of note, and a much respected leader in the field of Foreign Missions for his denomination, and although his children gained fame and prominence in their own right in several fields of their own choosing, he will be remembered and loved as the minister who brought the comfort of the Christian faith to his grief-stricken brother in the hour of his greatest sorrow by writing the words and music of "Near to the heart of God."

23.

ON JORDAN'S STORMY BANKS I STAND

When someone asked me half-seriously "Is 'On Jordan's Stormy Banks I Stand' the Baptist national anthem?" I had to laugh out loud, because there is no such thing as denominational national anthems in the first place, and if the Baptists of one particular country ever adopted one, or ever selected one special hymn for that honor, it would hardly be "On Jordan's Stormy Banks", although the author was about as much a Baptist as any man of his day or any subsequent day, for that matter.

When Rev. Samuel Stennett (1727-1795) wrote this famous hymn, he was thinking more of heaven than of baptism by immersion, and, although poetic references to the Jordan River sometimes imply baptism, that sacrament was farthest from Stennett's mind when he penned his historic stanzas for the 1787 edition of Rippon's "Baptist Selection". While the renowned Baptist clergyman was the contemporary of several of the "big six" of English hymnody (Isaac Watts, Philip Doddridge, Charles Wesley, John Newton, William Cowper and James Montgomery), he was never quite in their class as a hymn writer, although he excelled most of them as a preacher and pastor. When it came to writing a hymn on heaven, however, he thought in the same figures of speech as those utilized by the pioneer poet Rev. Isaac Watts so successfully.

Eighty years before Stennett sat down to write his hymn entitled "Heaven Anticipated", Watts wrote his under the caption "A prospect of Heaven makes death easy". Looking out over Southhampton water and England's famed Isle of Wight, Watts pictured himself standing beside Moses on Mt. Nebo, gazing in rapturous wonder over the beauty of the land of Canaan as it lay there beneath his feet, stretching from the Sea of Galilee on his right to the Dead Sea at his left, and from the banks of the Jordan River to the distant shores of the Mediterranean Sea. Viewing the landscape as Joshua must have seen it for the first time, centuries earlier, he wrote his hymn "There is a land of pure delight, Where saints immortal reign", in which he spoke of "Sweet fields beyond the swelling flood" that "Stand dressed in living green", little dreaming that a British Baptist would appropriate the lines of a staunch Anglican clergyman and include in his own hymn on heaven eighty years later these descriptive lines, "Sweet fields arrayed in living green, And rivers of delight!"

Christians of all ages have somehow pictured the Jordan River as the ancient Greeks did the River Styx, as the poetic barrier between earth and heaven, or the boundary line which separates this world from the next. And always, in their hymns and poems about the heavenly country, they imagined they were seeing it as Moses first gazed upon the land of Canaan, standing with his back to the east, facing the setting sun, and viewing the landscape through idealistic eyes that saw everything only in perfect hues, and pictured the reality as though it were a dream come true. Watts and Stennett were no exceptions, and were The Holy Land half as beautiful and fruitful as they pictured it in their hymns from the distance of thousands of miles and hundreds of years, Jacob and his party of seventy would never have abandoned it for the security and safety of Egypt during those early centuries of the Jewish era. In fact Stennett, who never visited Palestine, began his poem with the lines:

On Jordan's stormy banks I stand, And cast a wishful eye
To Canaan's fair and happy land, Where my possessions lie.

Years later a traveller stood in reality where Stennett had stood only in his imagination, and said, in surprise, to a fellow-traveller, "Why, the Jordan isn't stormy at all. It's rugged, but not stormy", a fact that could not be denied, which led some editors to alter Stennett's first line to conform with geographical certainties, and read, "On Jordan's rugged banks I stand."

Although the distinguished hymnologist, Rev. Samuel Duffield, defended this practice on the ground that it makes the hymn conform to that "dictate of modern taste which calls for truth as well as poetry in such sacred verses", "On Jordan's rugged banks" will never sound as familiar as "her Stormy banks", and, whether true or another illustration of poetic license, Christendom seems to be stuck with it from here on in!

Stennett, the preacher-poet, was such a talented young man that at one time he was filling the pulpits of two large Churches which had, in previous years, been served by his honored clergyman father, and his distinguished preacher grandfather, both of whom had borne the name, Rev. Joseph Stennett. When Samuel was twenty years of age, and had completed his education for the ministry, he became his father's assistant at the Baptist Church in Little Wild Street, Lincoln's Inn Fields, succeeding to the pulpit ten years later, in 1758, a position he filled with distinction until his death thirty-seven years later. Meantime, he was called to supply the pulpit of the Seventh Day Baptist Church in London, where his grandfather had preached for many years. Although he declined the call, he did agree to fill the pulpit, and he preached there every Saturday for more than twenty years. So if any man proved himself capable of writing a "Baptist national anthem" to order, Stennett was the man, since he was one of those rare and capable men of genius who could hold down two large pastorates simultaneously and in such an effective manner that neither congregation thought of discharging him in favor of the other!

For the same 1787 edition of Rippon's denominational hymnal, Stennett contributed his finest hymn, "Majestic Sweetness Sits Enthroned", having written it for a sermon "The Chiefest Among Ten Thousand, or The Excellence of Christ" some time before.

When first published, "On Jordan's Stormy Banks" was sung to several familiar Common Meter tunes. Later, when musicians took Isaac Watts' hymns, and rewrote them to lilting tunes with Choruses or Refrains, two men did the same thing with Stennett's hymn. Tullius C. O'Kane (1830-1912) a onetime professor at Ohio Wesleyan College, who set music to "The Home Over There" and other well-known gospel songs, prepared an original tune and added a Chorus of his own which read:

We will rest in the fair and happy land, Just across on the evergreen shore,
Sing the song of Moses and the Lamb, by and by, And dwell with Jesus evermore.

93

R. M. McIntosh did the same thing, only he came up with a Refrain that eventually became more popular than O'Kane's, for he sang in his Chorus these words:

I am bound for the Promised Land, I am bound for the Promised
 Land;
Oh, who will come and go with me, I am bound for the Promised
 Land.

No matter which tune one chooses, whether the dignified cadences of "Azmon",, "Avon" or "St. Agnes", or the lilting tunes of O'Kane and McIntosh, the perennial truths of Stennett's stanzas will continue to live, for in them he voiced the longings, hopes and aspirations of every Christian as he faces the mystery of death, expressing them in this manner:

O'er all those wide extended plains Shines one eternal day;
There God, the Sun, forever reigns, and scatters night away.
No chilling winds nor poisonous breath Can reach that healthful
 shore;
Sickness and sorrow, pain and death, Are felt and feared no more.
Filled with delight, my raptured soul Would here no longer stay;
Though Jordan's waves around me roll, Fearless I'd launch away!

24

ONE MORE DAY'S WORK FOR JESUS

Before her father, a prominent New York lawyer, lost most of his fortune in the financial panic of 1837, "work" to his youngest daughter, Anna Bartlett Warner, was merely a four letter word in the dictionary. But when she and her older sister Susan were forced out of their lavish Long Island home, and compelled to move to the Warner's recently purchased residence on Constitution Island, life suddenly took a different turn, and the two Warner girls and their father's sister, Aunt Fanny, re-established themselves at "Wood Crag" on this spot of land out in the Hudson River not too far from West Point, the seat of the United States Military Academy.

Susan and Anna soon learned that daily bread came as a result of daily work, and, with Aunt Fanny's encouragement, they began to make ceramics and invent games, and do many things with their hands which they had formerly considered too menial for their dainty fingers, and beneath the dignity of cultured and aristocratic young ladies of their social class.

When they had about exhausted their strength as well as their resources, Miss Fanny Warner, who made a home for her brother and his two lively, talented daughters following Mrs. Warner's death sometime before the economic crisis mentioned above, suggested that the girls collaborate in writing a book.

Undaunted, even though dreams of a successful literary career had never crept into either girl's imagination prior to that moment, Susan and Anna agreed to try. The result was that, several years later, Susan, in 1850, her thirty-first year, submitted to several publishers the manuscript of her first novel, "The Wide, Wide World".

Quite a few of them turned it down, but when the mother of George Putnam, head of the publishing house that bore his family name, read through the original manuscript, she insisted that her son publish it. Her feminine intuition never paid greater dividends, for Susan's premier publication outsold every other novel of its day with the sole exception of "Uncle Tom's Cabin" by Harriet Beecher Stowe.

Its widespread popularity is attested by the fact that the volume underwent numerous subsequent publications, the last edition coming out in 1920, seventy years and several generations after its initial publications in the middle of the nineteenth century.

Thus, having embarked so dramatically upon a literary career, Susan and Anna continued to write, to edit, to collaborate and to translate, until, at the time of Anna's death at the age of ninety-three, in 1915 (Susan having preceeded her in death in 1885), the two Warners had published more than seventy separate volumes on a wide variety of subjects.

Meantime, at their Constitution Island home, they entertained many classes of cadets from the Military Academy, their interest in that school dating from the days when their father's brother, Thomas Warner, had served as Chaplain and Professor there.

On Sunday afternoons they conducted a well-attended Sunday School class for the cadets in the well furnished living room of their island home that has been preserved as an historical shrine to this very day. It was while Anna was compiling material for her book "Hymns of the Church Militant" in 1858, that she became intrigued with the request of the Greeks who came to Philip, one of the twelve apostles, saying to him, "Sir, we would see Jesus" (John 12:21) and decided to write an original hymn based upon that phrase. The result was a hymn of seven stanzas, the first of which contained these lines:

> We would see Jesus; for the shadows lengthen
> Across the little landscape of our life;
> We would see Jesus, our weak faith to strengthen
> For the last weariness, the final strife.

Her last stanza was especially dramatic, as she wrote:

> We would see Jesus; this is all we're needing;
> Strength, joy and willingness come with the sight;
> We would see Jesus, dying, risen, pleading;
> Then welcome day, and farewell mortal night.

Inspired by this hymn, almost half a century later, College President J. Edgar Park took the Biblical phrase that had caught the attention of Anna Warner and wrote an entirely new hymn bearing identically the same title "We would see Jesus", in the first stanza of which he wrote:

> We would see Jesus; lo, his star is shining
> Above the stable where the angels sing;
> There in a manger on the hay reclining,
> Haste, let us lay our gifts before the King.

Strangely enough, Park's hymn is now sung to the tune "Cushman" which was composed in 1905 by Rev. Herbert B. Turner for Miss Warner's hymn, while he was serving as Chaplain at Virginia's Hampton Institute.

This is not the first instance of two well-known hymns bearing the same title. In 1887, the British poet, Marianne Hearn (1834-1909) wrote a hymn beginning "Just as I am, thine own to be" which was suggested to her by Charlotte Elliott's autobiographical hymn "Just as I am without one plea", which had been written half a century earlier.

Although as great an authority as Julian claims that the popular gospel hymn, "I want to be an angel" was written by a Miss Sidney P. Gill of Philadelphia, when one of her Sunday school pupils, Annie Louisa Farrant, said in class one Sunday morning, "Oh, I want to be an angel", the Warner sisters included an original hymn based upon that same title in their joint novel "Say and Seal" first published in 1859. Julian dates the little Miss Farrant's death, shortly after she made her unusual comment, as April 19, 1845, fourteen years prior to the Warner's version based upon the same phrase. It may have been a case of the Warner's being inspired by another's original phrase, just as Anna's hymn had been the inspiration of Park's years later.

In 1869 as she was preparing "Wayfaring Hymns Original and Translated", Anna Warner came across a letter written by Rev. Benjamin A. Adams, who wrote that at the close of an unusually busy and strenuous day he had found himself physically weary but abounding in spiritual joy. For him and other "Tired Servants", she wrote her hymn of encouragement under the caption "The Song of a Tired Servant" in which she exhorted her fellow Christians not to be weary in well-doing knowing they would "reap if they faint not".

One more day's work for Jesus, One less of life for me.
But heaven is nearer And Christ is dearer Than yesterday to me:
His love and light Fill all my soul tonight.

One more day's work for Jesus; O yes, a weary day;
But heaven shines clearer And rest comes nearer; At each step of the way;
And Christ is all, Before His face I fall.

Her sixth stanza concluded the hymn with these lines of assurance:

O blessed work for Jesus, O rest at Jesus feet.
There toil seems pleasure, My wants are treasure, And pain for him is sweet.
Lord, if I may, I'll serve another day.

Set to music by Rev. Robert Lowry, who wrote the words and music of "Shall we gather at the river" and "Christ arose", as well as the tunes for many fine hymns and gospel songs, this poem of Miss Warner's became quite popular, being included in such standard collections as those published by Moody and Sankey. She included in her novel "Say and Seal" a poem which became the finest hymn for Christian children that has ever been written, "Jesus loves me, this I know".

At her death, Constitution Island was willed to the United States government to become a permanent part of the West Point Military Academy. The two sisters are buried there at West Point, their graves being hallowed by the visits of hundreds of men and women, boys and girls, who wish to honor the memory of the women who gave to Christendom "Jesus bids us shine", "Jesus loves me", "I want to be angel", "We would see Jesus" and "One more day's work for Jesus".

25.

REVIVE US AGAIN

Among the Church leaders that Moody and Sankey met in the British Isles during their successful evangelistic services there during the last quarter of the nineteenth century was Dr. Horatius Bonar (1808-1889), the Free Church leader who is generally regarded as the greatest Scottish hymn-writer.

By the time Bonar shared his pulpit at Chalmers Memorial Church, Edinburgh, with the American evangelistic team, he had established himself as a vigorous thinker, a profound and moving preacher, and a gifted poet as well as a faithful pastor. Congregations were already singing his hymn "Go labor on, spend and be spent" which he had penned in 1836, as well as his surpassingly beautiful hymn written ten years later, "I heard the voice of Jesus say", dated 1846, the clergyman's thirty-eighth year.

Ira David Sankey (1840-1908), the musical member of the Moody-Sankey party, sought out every available new sacred poem that he felt had hymnic possibilities during his stay in Great Britain, setting the best ones to music as rapidly as he could. This insatiable curiosity resulted in his discovery of the poem that inspired his finest contribution to ecumenical hymnody, "The ninety and nine".

While reading through some of the works of Alfred Lord Tennyson, England's poetic genius and poet laureate, Sankey was deeply stirred by several stanzas included in the poet's "Guinevere", especially that portion that contained the sad lament "Late, late, so late, and dark the night and chill".

As was his custom, he immediately sat down at his little portable organ and composed a tune for those melancholy lines. But when he sought publication permission from the copyright owners of Tennyson's works, he ran into more trouble that he had anticipated, and when legal difficulties arose, he abandoned his original plan to include the new hymn in a forthcoming publication, and asked Dr. Bonar to come to his rescue by writing suitable stanzas to match the mood of the tune that had already been composed.

Undaunted, the famous Scotch divine rose to the occasion, and penned eight stanzas under the caption, "Yet there is room", the first of which contained these words:

"Yet there is room!" The Lamb's bright hall of song
With its fair glory beckons thee along; Room, room, still room!
O, enter, enter now!

While he was at it, Bonar did not stop with just one hymn but proceeded to write several more along the same general idea, one beginning, "Watch, brethren, watch", and the hymn that became the most successful of them all, "Rejoice and be glad". Written in 1875, this hymn was included in the 1875 edition of Sankey's "Sacred Songs and Solos", and was quickly accepted and sung to a stirring tune composed almost half a century earlier by John Jenkins Husband (1760-1825). In fact, the composer had been dead for fifty years before Bonar's seven stanzas were wedded to his music.

The composer, a native of Plymouth, England, had, after serving some time as a clerk at Surrey Chapel, England, migrated to the United States, arriving in 1809, at the age of forty-nine, spending his remaining years in Philadelphia, making his living as a music teacher as well as serving as the clerk of St. Paul's Episcopal Church.

The stanzas for which Husband originally composed his tune did not outlive their generation, but Bonar's lines quickly caught on and are included in the 1954 edition of the Methodist Hymn Book published in London for use among British Methodists, nearly three-quarters of a century after they were written.

In that volume Husband's tune is entitled "Rejoice and be glad" and its source is given as "Revival Tune Book, 1864". Bonar's opening stanza and chorus contained these lines:

Rejoice and be glad! the Redeemer hath come;
Go, look on His cradle, His cross and His tomb.
Sound His praises, tell the story, of Him who was slain;
Sound His praises, tell with gladness, He liveth again.

The mood of Husband's tune matched perfectly the joyous note of Bonar's poem, while the contagious enthusiasm of the "Refrain" made it difficult for some worshippers to believe that the lines came from the pen of the same minister who had written the Communion hymn "Here, O my Lord, I see Thee face to face", which Bonar had penned nearly twenty years prior to 1874. But the tune not only captured the imagination of Bonar and Sankey, it also gripped the heart of a third party who possibly never met either of the other two distinguished churchmen, although, he, like Bonar, was a Protestant clergyman.

Strangely enough, this third man, Rev. William Paton Mackay, wrote his new hymn eight years before Bonar wrote "Rejoice and be glad". And, whereas Bonar had been moved to write his new poem at Sankey's request, Mackay received his inspiration from two verses of Scripture. Whether he was merely reading through the Bible for his own spiritual enrichment or searching for a good text for a Sunday sermon, he soon came across this verse in the writings of one of the minor prophets of the Old Testament, Habakkuk 3:2, "O Lord, I have heard thy speech and was afraid; O Lord, revive thy work in the midst of the years, in the midst of the years made known; in wrath remember mercy."

Immediately Mackay recalled a similar verse in the Book of Psalms and quickly turned to Psalm 85:6, "Wilt thou not revive us again, that thy people may rejoice in thee?" Putting the two ideas together, Patton began to write:

> We praise Thee, O God, for the Son of Thy love,
> For Jesus who died and is now gone above.
> Hallelujah! Thine the glory, Hallelujah! Amen.
> Hallelujah! Thine the glory, Revive us again.

His second stanza praised God as "The Spirit of Light" and his third ascribed "All glory and praise to the Lamb that was slain", while his concluding lines were these:

> Revive us again, fill each heart with Thy love;
> May each soul be rekindled with fire from above.

Some years later, when Bonar had popularized Husband's tune with "Rejoice and be glad", Mackay realized that his stanzas could also be sung to Husband's music and that they actually possessed more evangelistic possibilities for congregational singing than the words then in general use. When he put the two together, he knew he had a success, and the response of the hymn-singing public quickly justified the wisdom of the poet's choice.

"Revive us again" spread more rapidly among the Christians in America than "Rejoice and be glad" had in the British Isles, and soon Churches of all denominations were making it their very own. As evangelists travelled the length and breadth of the expanding Republic, they carried it with them, and seldom was a series of Revival Services begun, in tabernacle, tent, country church or city cathedral, without the singing of Mackay's stanzas to Husband's music, with never a word of thanks thrown in to Bonar for having popularized the music in his own way in his own land.

While this popular gospel hymn may not be used as widely today as it was during the first half of the twentieth century, its message is just as pertinent now as it was then and the need for a revival of spiritual concern will continue to be one of the basic needs of every generation of every age, everywhere.

26

SAFE IN THE ARMS OF JESUS

When a Cincinnati, Ohio business man, Mr. William H. Doane, called at the New York City home of the famous hymnwriter, Fanny Crosby, one afternoon in the summer of 1868, the prolific blind poet little dreamed that his brief visit would inspire her to write one of her most popular gospel songs, and the one which she was to call "my favorite" for the rest of her long and active life.

Doane, a musician and song-leader as well as a successful industrialist from the Buckeye State, hastened to tell his hostess that he had only forty minutes in which to talk with her and then hurry to the railroad station to catch a train for home. He had already composed a stirring new hymn tune, he went on to explain, and wanted her to write some appropriate stanzas for his music, so he could introduce the new hymn at a state-wide Sunday School convention scheduled to be held in the Ohio metropolis the following month. Rushing to the piano, he played with intense feeling a thrilling piece of music and then turned and asked Fanny Crosby to do something about it right then and there. As he played, she wrote, and as he picked up his hat and started to say "Good-bye" she handed him a piece of paper on which she had just written her stanzas. En route to Cincinnati later that afternoon, Mr. Doane opened the piece of paper, and read for the first time the stanzas she had written to fit his music, the words of the famous gospel song "Safe In The Arms Of Jesus".

Following its introduction at the Sunday School convention the next month, it rapidly sang its way into the hearts and hymnals of Christendom, and soon the poet confessed that, of the more than eight-thousand hymns and songs she wrote, "Safe In The Arms Of Jesus" was her personal favorite.

Forty-one years after that memorable summer afternoon in 1868, my father, Rev. S. K. Emurian, composer, song-writer, singer, musician, preacher and lecturer, took as his bride Miss Grace Ruliffson Jenanyan, the eldest daughter of an honored Armenian clergyman, missionary and educator, Rev. Hartune S. Jenanyan, and his wife, Helene C. Ruliffson, whose family called her Nellie. Fanny Crosby often visited the Bowery Mission in New York City, where Nellie's father, Rev. Albert G. Ruliffson, the Mission's founder, was serving as director. The Ruliffsons and Fanny Crosby were close personal friends and the work at the Bowery Mission was especially dear to the poet's heart. In the present Bowery Mission Chapel in New York City is a memorial plaque to Pastor Ruliffson, which contains these words, "In loving memory of Rev. Albert G. Ruliffson, Founder of this Mission, November 1879, President of its Board of Trustees and active in its work until September 1895. Entered into Rest May 2nd, 1897. 'If any man serve me, him will my Father honor'. John 12:26."

"S.K.", a native of Armenia, who escaped to the United States in 1898, after receiving his A.B. degree at Anatolia College in Marsovan, Asia Minor, graduated with a Bachelor of Divinity from Oberlin, in Ohio, in 1901, whereupon he entered into evangelistic work, preaching and singing in Churches of many denominations throughout the north and northwest. He and his bride visited Round Lake, New York, a Methodist Assembly ground, on their honeymoon that July of 1909, and it was there that they met Fanny Crosby. Mother recorded that memorable event in the diary she kept that summer. Under the dateline, July 11, 1907, is this entry, "In the evening, Fanny J. Crosby told how she came to write many of her favorite hymns and stories. Very interesting. What a wonderful woman she is! Such childlike faith! Such sweet love, such cheerfulness. It put me to shame. She was pleased and surprised when I told her I was the grand-daughter of Rev. and Mrs. Ruliffson, and the daughter of Nellie Ruliffson (dear Mother). (Later she remembered that when she was introduced to Fanny Crosby, she said, "Aunt Fanny, do you remember Helene Ruliffson, called Nellie? Aunt Fanny I am Nellie's daughter," to which the sightless poet replied graciously, "Why, my dear, you look just like your Mother."

Fanny Crosby wrote an original poem, "To my friend, Nellie," for her 16th birthday, dated January 14, 1881, in Nellie's autograph album, now a cherished possession of the Emurian family.)

"For sixteen years she assisted Grandfather in the Bowery Mission. How dearly she loved Grandfather, Grandmother and Mother. Sisag won a warm place in her heart. His singing she appreciated very much. At the service he sang "Rescue the Perishing" in a sweet beautiful way." (This was the song she was inspired to write one night during a service at the Bowery Mission when Pastor Ruliffson was in the pulpit.) The very next day, Mother made this entry in her 'honeymoon diary'; July 12, 1909, "What a wonderful day this has been. Helpful messages came to me from the lecturers, and dear Aunt Fanny Crosby, A dear soul she is, how loving to Sisag and me. We shall miss her when she goes away. Aunt Fanny spoke this afternoon about great men she had known . . . . At 9 o'clock a reception was given for Aunt Fanny at 'The Orient'. A quartet (Sisag and I included) sang two of her hymns. She has carried us to the feet of Jesus. Our lives have been strengthened by meeting her."

The next day, my father had the honor of escorting Fanny Crosby to hear Dr. Russell Conwell deliver his famous lecture "Acres of Diamonds", the speech which built Temple University in Philadelphia. Mother wrote, "She was delighted and so were we."

"Her beautiful life has left a lasting impression on us. Sisag and I love her dearly. She spoke often of dear Mother, and her love for her is as sweet as ever, Auntie says. Sisag sang for her in Armenian 'Safe In The Arms Of Jesus', Auntie's favorite hymn, and several English hymns and songs. God bless her and us. Amen." On July 14, 1909, Fanny Crosby left Round Lake, and Mother wrote in her diary "How we missed her. Her cheerful life has taught us many lessons. Often she told me of her love for Mother. She kissed Sisag and me Goodbye and spoke a few comforting words. God bless her." Father recalled that a particularly blunt-speaking woman asked Fanny Crosby how it felt to be blind, to which the devout Christian woman replied graciously, "God closed these eyes (pointing to her physical eyes) that He might open these eyes" (pointing to the eyes of her heart), while Mother remembered her saying to the assembled throng at the

Summer Conference ground, "I am going to take the love of each one of you and lock it up here inside my heart, and then throw the key away."

In my parent's photograph album are several pictures of father and mother and Fanny Crosby taken during that visit at Round Lake, New York in July, 1909. Their paths never crossed again prior to Aunt Fanny's death in 1915 at the age of ninety-five, but father was privileged to compose tunes for several of her poems, and the influence of the Godly woman, who is now "Safe in the arms of Jesus", upon the lives of my parents, was a rich and rewarding one, and to me, looking back through the years, it was a high honor and providential privilege for two generations of our family to associate so intimately with one of the world's most unusual and one of Christendom's most remarkable women, Fanny J. Crosby (1820-1915).

27.

SOFTLY AND TENDERLY

Two famous gospel-song writers, Will Lamartine Thompson, (1847-1909), the "Bard of Ohio", and Fanny Crosby (1820-1915) one of the most prolific religious poets who ever lived, had one thing in common in addition to their genius for writing sacred verse. They both had the same kind of Christian experience. It was not the dramatic, sensational, earth-shaking type, which some professional evangelists hold up as the norm or the ideal, such as had blinded Paul and thrown him to the desert sands on the Damascus Road when he was "converted". Rather, it was a gradual, quiet, profound and yet personal experience, comparable to the call of Andrew by Jesus, or resembling His invitation to James and John to "Come, follow me". Both of them revealed this secret in a sacred song, Fanny Crosby confessing it in her popular stanzas "Jesus is tenderly calling thee home", and Will

Thompson asserting a similar truth in his most famous composition, "Softly and tenderly Jesus is calling".

The fact that both of them described the Master as calling His converts "tenderly" is indicative of the way each of them had heard His summons, and answered it. Unlike Thompson, Fanny Crosby, who was a poet and not a musician or composer, never made a fortune with her talent, although she did for fifty years fill a contract to supply one publisher with three hymns a week, for which she was paid a modest stipend. Thompson, who was gifted both as a poet and a composer, was regarded in his day as one of those rare men of genius who refused to starve to death in a stuffy little garrett just because he preferred to make a living as a musician. In fact, some of his critics spoke rather sarcastically of him as "that millionaire composer", a tribute that revealed more of their jealousy than his artistry. He had his share of business sense as well as innate talent, however, and refused to give away his songs when he felt they were worth paying for.

A resident of East Liverpool, Ohio, where he lived the greater part of his sixty-two years, although a native of Beaver County, Pa., and where he died, Thompson enrolled in the New England Conservatory of Music in Boston after graduating from Mount Union College, Alliance, Ohio. The son of strong Scotch-Irish Presbyterian parents, he early revealed that latent musical gift which was to earn him a substantial fortune in later years. Although he began composing as early as his sixteenth year, it was not until he was a maturing musician of twenty-eight that he considered offering some of his original songs for publication. That year, 1875, he polished off four new compositions, and promptly offered them to a Cleveland music publisher for the sum of $100. Such a sum being an unheard of payment for the songs of a relatively unknown beginner and a novice in the publishing game, the Cleveland businessman introduced the young musician to the "dog-eat-dog" world of publishers by offering him $25 for all four, admonishing him that "such material can be had in abundance free of charge".

Undaunted, Thompson refused the generous offer, tucked his manuscripts under his arm and bided his time until a more propitious moment arrived. Some time later, when in New York City on a business trip for his father, Josiah Thompson, an East

Liverpool drygoods merchant, Will arranged for the publication of his songs on his own. Three of them enjoyed fair popularity, "Drifting with the tide", "My home on the old Ohio", and "Under the moonlit sky", but one skyrocketed to success, and became the day's most successful song, "Gathering Shells from the seashore".

The printing presses were compelled to run night and day to supply the demand, and Will soon had the last laugh on the unfortunate publisher who turned down a small fortune because he hesitated to invest $100 in a new song writer's initial offerings.

Inspired by his unexpected good fortune, Thompson established his own Music Company in Chicago, turning out popular, patriotic and semi-sacred songs, as well as collections of hymns, anthems and concert pieces for general use, books which were reputed to have had a combined sale of nearly two-million copies.

In addition, he managed a music store in East Liverpool for over a quarter of a century, personally supervising the loading of wagons with organs and pianos and marketing them all over the adjacent country side. If he found a customer curious but undecided, he often played and sang for several hours while softening up the prospect and clinching a sale.

Through the courtesy of Mr. John D. Raridan, of The Brush-Moore Newspapers, Canton, Ohio, this writer came into possession of many facts about the life and creative work of Will Thompson who was regarded as one of Columbiana County's most renowned citizens. Thompson, a Republican and a Mason, married Elizabeth, the daughter of Dr. and Mrs. Robert Johnson of Wellsville, Ohio, to which union one son, Leland, was born.

When the Master "tenderly" touched his heart, Will Thompson turned to the writing and composing of religious music, a field in which he proved as preeminent as those he had already conquered. His love for the grand old hymns of Zion and his appreciation of their ministry is seen in his sacred composition, "The Sinner and the Song" in which he used the strains of several of the majestic hymns he had known from childhood. No finer testimony to the power of the Christian gospel can be found than in Thompson's autobiographical gospel hymn "Jesus is all the world to me, My life, my joy, my all", a perennial favorite of believers around the world. His "Lead me gently home, Father", has that note of certainty and assurance which is the proudest possession of the children of God. But he riched his zenith when he pictured the Master, like the father of the prodigal son, pleading patiently and yet earnestly, for his wayward boy to come back home. Pouring all of the richness and beauty of his own Christian faith in his stanzas, and wedding them to a tune that was lyrical and yet emotionally moving and mellowing, he wrote the words and music of his finest gospel hymn, which began:

Softly and tenderly Jesus is calling, Calling for you and for me;
See on the portals He's waiting and watching, Watching for you
    and for me.
Come home, come home, Ye who are weary, come home;
Earnestly, tenderly, Jesus is calling, Calling, O sinner, come home.

Years later, when the world-renowned lay preacher, Dwight Lyman Moody, lay on his death bed in his Northfield, Massachusetts home, Will Thompson made a special visit to inquire as to his condition. The attending physician refused to admit him to the sickroom, and Moody heard them talking just outside the bedroom door. Recognizing Thompson's voice, he called for him to come to his bedside. Taking the Ohio poet-composer by the hand, the dying evangelist said, "Will, I would rather have written 'Softly and tenderly Jesus is calling' than anything I have been able to do in my whole life'."

Although his popular songs earned him treasures on earth, Will Thompson had the satisfaction of knowing, prior to his death in 1909, that his noblest sacred hymn had earned him "treasures in heaven, where neither moss nor rust doth corrupt, and where thieves do not break through nor steal."

28

SOMEDAY HE'LL MAKE IT PLAIN

Some people can take tragedy in their stride and never for a fleeting moment question the goodness and love of their kind Heavenly Father. Other people even express a willingness to "drink the bitter cup" in order to prove to themselves as well as to their God the quality and depth of their devotion.

Such a Christian was Jennie Evelyn Hussey, the gospel hymn writer who was born in Henniker, New Hampshire, February 8, 1874. This devout child of consecrated Quaker parents began writing poetry at the age of seven, although she was unable to find a publisher for her works until many years and numerous poems later. After spending most of her life in her ancestral home, she went to live in the "Home for the Aged" in Concord, New Hampshire, where, despite the afflictions of neuritis, she continued writing the joyful lyrics that characterized her younger and happier days.

It was in her most popular gospel hymn "Lead me to Calvary" that she wrote this poetic prayer as the fourth and final stanza:

"May I be willing, Lord, to bear Daily the cross for Thee;
Even Thy cup of grief to share, Thou hast borne all for me,"

and apparently she wrote more prophetically than she realized at the time.

Still other believers have a difficult time trying to reconcile un-merited, unexpected and undeserved trials and tribulations with the Christian concept of a beneficent and merciful God, and, when sudden sorrows descend upon the soul, they have a hard time bearing or even accepting them. The natural spirit of re-bellion quickly overcomes all thoughts of God's love and His considerate and compassionate Providence while all hope is seem-ingly washed away in the flood of tears that follows.

It was just such a soul-shattering experience that plumeted the faith of the brilliant composer Adam Geibel to the depths of despair. Geibel, a native of Germany, where he had been born in 1885, had migrated to the United States as a young lad, more in search of freedom than fortune, but his innate musical talent as well as his early training stood him in good stead in his adopted country, and before very long the Adam Geibel Music Company was publishing sacred and popular successes with enviable monotony.

This was all the more remarkable in view of the fact that Adam was totally blind, having lost his sight as a result of a serious eye infection that afflicted him when he was eight years of age. Like blind Fanny Crosby (1820-1915) the prolific American author of thousands of gospel hymns and songs, and Rev. George Matheson, the distinguished blind Presbyterian clergyman of Edinburgh, Scotland ("O Love That Wilt Not Let Me Go"), he developed that "second-sight" which enabled him to perceive with the eyes of the heart and mind what many others failed to see with their physical sight. Sudden tragedy struck the Geibel family when their only daughter's husband, a foreman in a steel mill, lost his life in a horrible accident when an explosion destroyed a portion of the mill in which he had been working at the time. When the distraught father recalled the bright promises that the future had held for the recently married young couple, his grief became almost inconsolable.

Try as he might, he could not reconcile his understanding of the God that Jesus revealed with the purposeless agony to which he and his family were then being subjected. His spiritual pain was all the more acute when he remembered that his son-in-law had been a radiant and magnetic Christian.

Seeking to find solace in the consoling words of comforting friends, Geibel went to the home of a fellow-composer of sacred music, C. Austin Miles ("In The Garden"), and poured out his heart. In their conversation he related an experience that had come to him the previous night, when, lying sleepless in bed brooding over his personal sorrow and his daughter's distress, he had suddenly heard a voice saying, "Child, you do not understand it now, but some day you'll understand; some day it will all be plain!"

Geibel told Miles that he had cried out in answer, making the words the distraught father of a demon-possessed son had spoken to the Lord, his very own words, "Yes, Lord, I believe, help Thou mine unbelief! I know that Thou wilt make it plain to me some day!" It was at that precise moment that a beautiful melody flowed into the heart and mind of the blind musician as if God, in answer, lovingly crowded out all thoughts of bitterness and pain.

The following day, Adam wrote out his music and a rough idea of the stanzas he felt would be appropriate, and mailed his manuscript to Mrs. Lida Shivers Leech at her New Jersey home, requesting her to edit his lines and add some lines of her own to complete the poem he needed.

A native of Mayville, New Jersey, where she was born July 12, 1873, Mrs. Leech had studied music since her tenth year, although she had not penned a salable poem until she was thirty-five, though many of the most important events of her life were closely connected with familiar hymns and gospel songs. The first hymn she ever played in public in Sunday School was "Whiter Than Snow", and the hymn "Hallelujah, 'Tis Done" was being sung by a Church choir when she went forward to dedicate her life to Christ and unite with the Methodist Church as a young girl of twelve.

Although publishers rejected her early writings on the ground that they were either too trite or too hackneyed, her pastor encouraged her to continue, and her practice perfected her in the art of writing acceptable poetry and singable music, "God's Way Is The Best Way" (copyrighted 1911) being among her finest original gospel hymns.

She complied with Geibel's request and sent him a poem that he soon returned, since it failed to meet his rather rigid requirements. Again she penned several stanzas to match his music, only to have that manuscript come back in the mail almost as soon as she had posted it. Undaunted, she tried a third time, but still to no avail. With the graciousness and perseverance born of many a previous heartache and disappointment, she tackled her problem for what proved to be the fourth and final time.

When Adam Geibel saw her stanzas, he was satisfied, for, as he read them, it seemed as if he himself had written them:

"I do not know why oft' 'round me, My hopes all shattered seem
    to be;
God's perfect plan I cannot see — But some day I'll understand."

The poet's affirmation of faith continued through the second
stanza which saw the tragedy as a time of testing one's faith in
and love for God, and the third in which she spoke of the praise
that would fill her life despite unexpected trials, since God still
led even through darkened days.

The song was quickly published in 1911 and became almost
immediately popular, the Copyright being renewed by The Rodeheaver Company twenty-eight years later, in 1939, as the song
was still in demand.

Adam Geibel wrote many more acceptable tunes, from the
popular male quartet melody "Kentucky Babe" to the stirring
strains of his new tune for "Stand Up For Jesus" prior to his
death in Philadelphia on August 3, 1933.

No doubt all of his questions were answered within a short
time after he had been translated from this earth to the Church
triumphant, when the "day" of which Mrs. Leech had sung in
her Chorus finally arrived:

"Someday He'll make it plain to me; Some day when I His face
    shall see;
Someday from tears I shall be free, For some day I shall under-
    stand."

29.

SOMEBODY'S PRAYING FOR YOU

The fact that she felt in her heart that somebody was praying
for her during her painful illness sustained Ida L. Reed when
everything else failed. Left a partial invalid at fifteen when an epidemic of diphtheria ravaged the residents of her mountain community a few miles from Philippi, West Virginia, she had been

further burdened when her father died of tuberculosis while still a fairly young man, and the responsibility of taking care of her half-sick mother and managing their little farm were suddenly thrown upon her. She could never have made the grade without the sustaining power of her deep and devout Christian faith. Just when a silver lining appeared in her cloudy sky, or just as she caught a glimpse of a rainbow shining through the rain, another cloud would appear to blot out the sun and wipe away the rainbow, and life would be dark and gloomy all over again.

But she read eagerly and avidly everything she could lay her hands upon and the magazines and books and journals that found their way to her humble hillside home were read and devoured from cover to cover. As she grew into older adolescence she cherished many a secret dream deep down inside her own heart, dreams that she dared not share even with her closest relative or dearest friend. For Ida L. Reed wanted to leave the narrow confines of her mountain community and go away to college in some romantic place where all of her youthful dreams could come true and all of her longings could be realized. For three cold and icy winters when snow covered the ground and mud filled the narrow roadways, Miss Reed fought back the tears and taught in a district school, saving every penny possible for that college education.

But the dream was shattered almost before it began, and the young student of twenty bundled up her school books, wrapped up her few personal possessions, wiped away the tears of disappointment that kept overflowing down her sunscarred cheeks, and boarded the train that would take her back to her home in the hidden and silent hills of West Virginia. Two physicians had refused to admit her to college because of the frailty of her health, pronouncing her "physically unable to continue her studies."

Heart-broken and in deep despondency, she wrote "All the long struggle of the past, with its broken dreams, thwarted plans and dead hopes, rose before me. I went down on my face before God, crushed and helpless; and in that black bitter hour I seemed to hear a Voice comforting me, promising me a greater blessing than that which I had lost — a fuller life of more blessed service."

Little did those two doctors know that God would not call Ida L. Reed (1865-1951) home until she had passed her eighty-fifth birthday! Disappointment led to a recurrence of the physical ailments that were to plague her for the rest of her life, and it was during one of those periods of intense bodily suffering coupled with unusual spiritual distress and mental confusion that the words flashed into her mind, "Somebody's praying for you." By that time she had already tried her hand at writing hymns and songs and occasional poems, having started when she dashed off a few simple rhymes for her school children to sing to several familiar melodies. One poem led to another, and soon, at the urgent insistence of her brother, she was mailing some of them out to various religious and secular periodicals.

To her amazement, requests for more poems began to come in the mails, accompanied by checks for a dollar or two dollars, stimulus enough for a poor mountain girl to write her heart out, if necessary. That night, fearful lest she lose consciousness, or that the phrase that had appeared out of nowhere might be forgotten before morning, she added additional words and then phrases and soon lines were giving way to lines, and almost before she knew it, another new song was being born out of her agony and pain.

When the dawn of the next day finally broke with its healing ministry of sunshine and fresh air, Ida L. Reed managed to write down her new poem, the first stanza containing these words:

"Come to the Father, O wanderer come, Somebody's praying for you;
Turn from the sin-paths, no longer to roam, Somebody's praying for you.
Somebody loves you wherever you stray, Bears you in faith to God day after day;
Prayerfully follows you all the dark way, Somebody's praying for you."

A publisher proudly paid her two dollars for the three stanzas and turned them over to Mr. C. Austin Miles (whose most popular song is "In The Garden"), who set them to music with hardly a thought of the prayers Ida Reed needed back in her West Virginia home.

And so the years passed, and Ida Reed wrote "I belong to the King", which became the official song of many Circles of King's Daughters, and was published in nearly four million hymnals and songbooks, and "I Cannot Drift Beyond Thy Love, Beyond Thy Tender Care" and about two thousand more hymns and songs on a wide variety of subjects for nearly every possible occasion. In addition, she taught herself to play the little organ she bought with some of her "royalties", and corresponded with Ira D. Sankey ("The Ninety and Nine"), Fanny Crosby ("Safe In The Arms Of Jesus") and Hart P. Danks ("Silver Threads Among The Gold") and other prominent hymn writers and composers of the day, despite the fact that stark poverty always stared her in the face, and the passing of the years brought no relief from the financial strain under which she had lived so long.

Then, Mr. Herman Johnson, a reporter for a Wheeling, West Virginia newspaper, The Intelligencer, wrote a story about the state's most prolific poet, and her condition of dire want. Shortly after that, his account was called to the attention of a field representative for ASCAP (American Society of Composers, Authors, and Publishers) who was discussing business matters with a theatrical man in that neighbourhood. Then Miss Beatrice Plumb spread the story of Ida L. Reed in the "Christian Herald" family magazine, with the result that from far and wide interested and generous people wrote in offering to help out in any way possible to make the seventy-four year old song writer's last years cheerful and bright. Richard Maxwell, with whom this columnist collaborated in two published songs, "Jonah And The Whale" and "You Can Do Anything", featured an Ida Reed song on his popular radio program, and included one in his latest book of hymns and songs.

Dr. H. Augustine Smith of Boston University, (who graciously assisted this writer by endorsing his first book back in 1941, assuring the publisher that he would not be bringing out "a failure" and starting me on the road to writing more books in the intervening years), was asked to state whether he would certify that Miss Ida L. Reed had made "a substantial contribution to American music". As a happy result, ASCAP, in keeping with the slogan stated by Victor Herbert when he and his associates organized the American Society of Composers, Authors and Publishers many years ago, "No man or woman in America who writes successful music shall ever want", voted her a monthly check for the rest of her life, although she was never a member of the

Society. They began this generous contribution in December 1939, and continued to supply her with much-needed and deeply-appreciated funds until her death on July 8, 1951. That it was a matter of national interest is attested by the fact that Kate Smith made an announcement to that effect on her nationwide radio broadcast as soon as this action had been taken.

So, all along, somebody must have been praying for Ida L. Reed just as she had been praying for somebody else, and the loving God, Father of us all, who hears all our prayers on behalf of all of His children, listened and, in His own way, answered, and the heart of this dear woman was gladdened in the evening time of her life with the assurance that she had not been forgotten, neither by her Heavenly Father nor by those whom she had placed in her debt by her hymns and gospel songs.

30.

SOMETIME WE'LL UNDERSTAND

The collaboration of two Pennsylvania farm boys by means of an interested third party resulted in the popular gospel song "Sometime We'll Understand". Unfortunately this familiar song is heard more often today at funerals where the deceased are memorialized than at religious services for the inspiration of the living for whom it was originally intended.

The first farm lad from "Penn's Woods" was Maxwell Newton Cornelius, a native of Allegheny County in the western part of the state, where he was born on July 30, 1842. Although he was raised on a farm, he forsook that calling as soon as he was old enough, and took up carpentry. The success which attended his youthful efforts encouraged him to venture still further into the business world, as a result of which he became a building contractor.

Phil Kerr is the authority for the story that it was while Cornelius was busy in the building business that an accident occurred, as a tragic result of which the contractor's leg was so badly broken and mangled that an immediate amputation was ordered by the attending physician. Since no anesthetic was available, the operation proceeded in spite of the fact that the patient was fully conscious throughout the trying ordeal.

It was sometime after this unforseen turn of events that the successful business man "sought the Lord" and felt called of God to follow the invitation of the Carpenter of Nazareth, and prepare himself for the Christian ministry. The "General Biographical Catalogue of the Western Theological Seminary of the Presbyterian Church, 1827-1927" states that after attending Vermillion Institute in Ohio in 1867, Cornelius entered that seminary, receiving his degree in 1871, his twenty-ninth year. He was licensed and ordained as a Presbyterian clergyman following the commencement exercise in May, 1871, becoming a member of the Pittsburgh Presbytery of the Presbyterian Church, U.S.A. (the Northern branch of Presbyterianism in The United States) assuming his first pastorate at the Oakdale, Pennsylvania, Presbyterian Church.

After a two-year ministry there, during which he also served as "Stated Supply and Pastor" of the Valley Church, he was called to the pulpit of the Presbyterian Church in Altoona, where he served for nine years, 1876-1885.

The newspaper editorials that urged ambitious young men to "go west" must have caught the maturing minister's imagination, for, after a fruitful pastorate in Altoona he accepted a call from a small Church with a great future in Pasadena, California. Although his obituary notice which appeared in the Washington, D.C. "Evening Star" of April 1, 1893, stated that he went from a Church in San Francisco to serve the Pasadena congregation, his biographical sketch in the Seminary publication gives his Pasadena years as 1885-1890 and his San Francisco pastorate as 1890-1891, which, more than likely, conforms more closely to the facts.

Beginning with a congregation of one-hundred faithful souls in Pasadena, Maxwell Newton Cornelius within three years had increased his membership ten-fold, at the same time carrying out plans for enlarging the Church's facilities and expanding her activities to such an extent that, in that brief period of time, the value of the Church's physical plant increased from $5,000 to $100,000, a truly remarkable achievement on the part of any pastor and congregation in any state of the Union at any time during her history.

Kerr continues his brief narrative of Cornelius' life and works with the account of a business depression that set in shortly after the spacious and expensive new Church sanctuary had been completed. As a result of the unexpected economic collapse, many members were unable to pay their pledges to the building fund, and soon a spirit of despondency began to creep through the congregation.

Coupled with that burden, the pastor had the added responsibility of a sick wife, whose rapidly declining health demanded that he devote more and more of his time and energy to her care and comfort. It was during this period in his life shortly before the last decade of the nineteenth century, that he was moved to pen the only poem that bears his name that found a place in the hymnals and songbooks of Christendom.

While he was personally striving to understand the mind of God and the purposes of God in permitting so many tragic events to pile up one upon another until he felt he could not bear the load any longer, he suddenly realized that in "God's better land", beyond the reach of sorrow and tears, God's children would understand everything, clearly, completely and convincingly. With those thoughts in his mind and heart, he wrote several stanzas, the first of which contained this affirmation of his unflinching faith:

"Not now, but in the coming years, It may be in the better land, We'll read the meaning of our tears, And there, sometime, we'll understand."

His autobiographical stanzas spoke of "catching the broken thread again" and "finishing what we here began" and wondering why so many of earth's plans were doomed to failure and so many of her songs ceased before they "scarce began".

Little dreaming that he was writing a gospel hymn, Maxwell Cornelius finished his five stanzas. When his wife died shortly thereafter, he himself conducted her funeral service, reading his new poem during his memorial sermon.

Some months later the stanzas appeared in the columns of a local newspaper, and among those who read them was Major Daniel Webster Whittle, a Massachusetts native who was two years Cornelius' senior. For several months he kept a copy in his possession until he met the second Pennsylvania farm boy, James McGranahan (1840-1907), his co-worker in the evangelistic field for nearly a decade, since the two men had met for the first time near Ashtabula, Ohio, at the scene of the terrible train wreck that took the life of the famous singer and composer, Philip Paul Bliss, on December 29, 1876. Whittle told McGranahan that he had added a chorus of his own to Cornelius' stanzas and that he wanted him to compose an appropriate tune.

McGranahan quickly complied, and when the words and music appeared in one of Sankey's "Gospel Hymns" collections, copyrighted 1891, it was under the Scripture verse "What I do thou knowest not now; but thou shalt know hereafter", John 13:7.

Following his Pasadena pastorate, Cornelius served Howard Church, San Francisco for one year before accepting a call to serve the Eastern Presbyterian Church, Washington, D.C. in 1891. After an all-too-brief three year pastorate in the nation's capitol, he died of pneumonia after a fortnight's illness, at his residence at 611 Maryland Avenue, at 4:25 P.M. on March 31, 1893.

His obituary stated that "he remained conscious up to the last and bore his trouble with true Christian fortitude. His deathbed was surrounded by the members of his family and a number of devoted friends from his congregation. He seemed almost to prolong his life for a while by sheer force of will and when he realized that the end was at hand, he requested Rev. Mr. Alden, the assistant at the Church, to sing for him, and the soul of the faithful minister passed away to the music of a well-loved hymn. His end was in keeping with the life of Christian usefulness that he had lived."

"He was survived by two daughters. During his ministry in Washington, he had succeeded in building up membership of the church to 'flattering proportions' and one good result of his labors was shown in the handsome, new and commodious church building that was all but completed for the use of the growing congregation at the time of the pastor's death. Rev. Dr. Hamlin and Rev. Dr. Barlett, co-workers in the Lord's vineyard, conducted his funeral services, after which his remains were taken to Ohio for interment." By that time, however, the preacher-poet had fulfilled the dream of which he had sung in the final stanza of his only famous gospel hymn:

"God knows the way, He holds the key; He guides us with unerr-
    ing hand;
Sometime with tearless eyes we'll see; Yes, there, up there, we'll
    understand."

31.

SUNRISE

An Associated Press release dated Friday, September 5, 1958, carried this news story from Warsaw, Indiana, "B. D. Ackley, pianist and Gospel song writer, died Wednesday at the age of 85. Mr. Ackley, who was in failing health for several years, held the title of music editor of the Rodeheaver Publishing Company at nearby Winona Lake. He had traveled all over the world as pianist for famed evangelists, including the late Billy Sunday. Mr. Ackley composed more than 3,500 Gospel songs, perhaps the best known of which were "Sunrise" and "If Your Heart Keeps Right"."

Bentley D. Ackley, who was born at Spring Hill, Pennsylvania, September 27, 1872, was the son of a Methodist father who himself was musically gifted. Quite early he accompanied his father on teaching trips, playing both the piano and the portable organ. When he mastered several wind and brass instruments, he played in his father's fourteen-piece band. He went to New York in 1888, studying stenography while serving as organist of a Brook-lyn Church. This training stood him in good stead when he joined Billy Sunday's evangelistic team as joint secretary-pianist, working with Sunday for eight years. Although he published his first song in 1892, it was not until his association with the Sunday School movement that he began writing prolifically in the field of gospel song. His brother, Alfred H. Ackley, fifteen years his junior, collaborated with B.D. in writing, composing and editing in this very same field, his best sacred song being the Easter favorite, "He Lives".

The immediate inspiration for B. D. Ackley's tune for the gospel hymn "Sunrise", which the Associated Press release mentioned as one of his finest and best-known musical compositions, was a religious poem from the pen of a beloved pastor of the Wilmington Conference of the Methodist Church, Rev. William Charles Poole. This writer of the stanzas of several popular gospel hymns and songs was born near Easton, Talbot County, Maryland on April 14, 1875, the son of William Charles and Rachel R. Poole, spending his early years on the family farm. His Godly family was connected with the local Methodist Church, and William attended the Sunday School and Church services with them regularly, finally uniting with the Church along with his brother, when he was a lad of eleven, in 1886.

Following the completion of his elementary and high school education, he entered Washington College in Chestertown, Maryland, graduating with his well-earned degree in 1899. The very next year he applied for membership in the Wilmington Conference of the Church of his choice, and was received during the sessions of the Conference which were held at Epworth Church, when Bishop Andrew was the presiding Bishop of that area. Thus began a remarkable career that saw the young clergyman develop his many talents as a soul-winner, a pastor, a preacher, a Church-financier, a contributor to numerous religious journals, a wide traveller and principally, a writer of gospel hymns and songs, a career that extended for the next thirty-six full and fruitful years.

When asked his personal definition of a good minister, Poole explained that a "good minister should be an effective soul-winner, compassionate pastor and a forceful preacher". To him the Methodist pioneer, Francis Asbury, was the ideal, and he often remarked that a perfect preacher would have to be "as industrious as Asbury, as sane as John Wesley, as gifted a preacher as George Whitfield, with a heart as big as that of the lay-evangelist Dwight L. Moody, who would keep out of debt, and be pure, patient and simple with others as Jesus was."

The alumni secretary of Poole's Alma Mater wrote that some of his pastoral appointments were: Mt. Salem M. E. Church, Wilmington, Delaware; the M. E. Church at Parsonsburg, Maryland; and St. John's Methodist Church, Lewisville, Pennsylvania. Early in his ministry, Poole utilized his gift of writing sacred poetry, and soon many of his stanzas were set to music and included in various publications of different religious music publishing houses.

In 1908 his hymn "Just When I Need Him Most," with a fine tune composed by Charles Gabriel, was copyrighted and published. Of the composer, the poet later said, "Without his encouragement, I might never have entered this field of service for God." In 1911, he wrote a sequel to the aforementioned hymn, entitling it "Just Where He Needs Me Most" which Gabriel again set to music, although it never attained the popularity of the earlier song. In 1914, he brought out "The Call of the Christ Rings Out Today", to another stirring Gabriel tune, while 1915 saw "Did You Pray Till the Answer Came" published to a tune by B. D. Ackley. When he came into contact with many business men in his several pastoral appointments, and realized most of them were country boys who had come to town and forgotten the Church of their fathers, he wrote "The Church By The Side of the Road" in 1925, which Ackley again set to a successful tune.

It was during a Methodist Conference session of the Wilmington Conference in the early nineteen-twenties that he heard a phrase which he was to immortalize in his finest gospel hymn. The song-leader for that particular session was another Rodeheaver co-worker, Mr. George W. Sanville, who was managing a successful publishing business when Homer Rodeheaver met up with him. In order to employ him, Rodeheaver had to buy out Sanville's company, but he later confessed that that deal was one of the finest investments he ever made. The two men became loyal and faithful friends from that moment on. Sanville recalled later that one of the older pastors at that Conference session spoke of his forthcoming retirement in these moving words, "The end of my days here is not sunset for me, but sunrise!"

That was all the inspiration that Rev. William C. Poole, a brother pastor sitting nearby, needed, and soon he had completed the three stanzas and chorus of a new sacred song which began with these lines:

"When I shall come to the end of my way, When I shall rest at the close of life's day,
When 'Welcome Home' I shall hear Jesus say, O that will be sunrise for me."

When B. D. Ackley composed his music a short while later, copyrighting it in 1924, the song began its ministry that was to take it to the far places of the earth, with its insistent note of the assurance of immortality, which is one of every Christian's spiritual possessions.

In addition to Mr. Ackley, Poole worked with other composers, including J. Lincoln Hall, Haldor Lillenas, C. Austin Miles and E. O. Excell. Late in his life, on September 12, 1945, he was united in marriage with a teacher from Easton, Maryland, Miss Grace Holmes. After four happy years together, this union was broken when Brother Poole died at Beebe Hospital, Lewes, Delaware, December 24, Christmas Eve, 1949, as the result of an accidental fall suffered several weeks before. His widow closed his Memorial to the Methodist Annual Conference with these words, "God called him to the Land of 'Eternal Sunrise', to spend Christmas with his loved ones there."

If Ackley and Poole did no more than give Christendom this one gospel hymn, their ministries of composing and writing were eminently worthwhile, for what nobler witness could a believer make than to close his life to this Refrain:

"Sunrise tomorrow; Sunrise tomorrow; Sunrise in glory is waiting for me;
Sunrise tomorrow; Sunrise tomorrow; Sunrise with Jesus for eternity."

32.

TAKE THE NAME OF JESUS WITH YOU

"Each name in the Bible has a certain meaning peculiar to itself," Mrs. Lydia Baxter told her friends as they were visiting in the living room of her New York City home, one afternoon in 1870. "For example, the name 'Jacob' was descriptive of the character of Jacob, because the name itself actually means 'Supplanter', since Jacob tried to supplant his twin brother, Esau, and be the first-born of the family rather than the second-born. You recall that when Esau was born Jacob had hold of Esau's heel, as if he were trying to pull his twin brother back so he could be born first. Consequently, he was named 'The Supplanter' for that very reason. Now the name 'Isaac' means 'laughter', for when Abraham and Sara learned that, at their advanced ages, they were to become parents, they laughed out loud, thinking it was impossible as well as incredible. As for the names of the twelve sons of Jacob, after whom most of the twelve tribes of Israel took their names, they were named for the strange events surrounding their birth, as well as the rivalries which existed between the wives of husband and father Jacob. 'Samuel' means 'Asked of God' since his mother Hannah asked God for a son, promising to dedicate the lad to God's service if only he would answer her prayer. He answered it, and she did what she had promised. 'Hannah' means 'grace' while 'Sarah' means princess, and 'Naomi' means pleasantness," she concluded.

Mrs. Baxter, despite her radiant personality and cheerful disposition, had long been an invalid and periodically was confined to her bed for days at a time. But those who came within the influence of her lovely Christian spirit, marveled at the way she bore her pain, endured her physical agony, and refused to let it crush her or make her any less Christian. For that reason, they came to visit her constantly, not so much to give her encouragement and comfort, as to receive from her some added bouyancy for themselves.

"Lydia," one of her most intimate friends used to confess, "We are not here to cheer you up. You don't need cheering up, but we do. And we are here so you, the sick one, can give us a little of your zest and so some of your wonderful faith can rub off on the rest of us."

She would smile, trying to ignore those flattering words, and quickly turn the conversation to another topic of common interest.

"How do you do it?" others would ask, as they marvelled at the way she triumphed over pain and confinement.

"I have some very special armour," she would reply.

"A secret weapon?" her friends would jokingly ask.

"Oh, no," she would say. "You see, I have the name of Jesus, and I use that name as my special protection. When the tempter tries to make me blue or despondent, I mention the name of Jesus, and he can't get through to tempt me any more. When I feel badly, and wonder if I will ever enjoy a good night's sleep again, I take the name of Jesus and ask him to give me the sooth- ing balm of his presence, and I soon drop off to sleep. The name 'Jesus' means Saviour and it comes from the same Hebrew root from which the names Joshua and Joash come. When I remem- ber that, and all that the name of Jesus signifies about the nature of personality of God, I can conquer any foe." Her life gave evidence of the reality of her faith, and soon her friends were searching the Scriptures to find out more about the name of Jesus which was so precious to their mutual friend and fellow Church member.

Lydia Baxter had been born in Petersburg, New York, Sep- tember 2, 1809. When she and her sister were converted as a result of the preaching of a Baptist missionary, they were both instrumental in organizing a Baptist Church in their home town. Following Lydia's marriage to Mr. Baxter, she and her husband moved to New York City, where they were to make their home until Mrs. Baxter's death, June 22, 1874.

Her friendship with many of the leading evangelists and their songleaders soon made her home a gathering place for Christian workers, and encouraged her to contribute her small services to the expanding evangelistic movement of her day by writing original hymns and poems for use in these public services of worship and praise. "While I cannot attend these services, I can help revive those who can by writing hymns and songs for their use," she confessed.

Her study of the Bible enabled her to understand the significance of the name of Jesus and appreciate its meaning and power in a wonderful way. "The name of Jesus represents the personality and character of Jesus in all his mighty power," she stated to her companions and fellow Bible students. "When Jesus stated that where 'two or three are gathered in my name' he meant that they were assembled together in his spirit for the purpose of glorifying him and expanding his work in the world. When the people shouted on Palm Sunday when he made his triumphal entry into Jerusalem 'Blessed is he who comes in the name of the Lord', they meant that Jesus came as the Lord, for the name represented the character of the Lord. Christians were those who 'believed on his name', which was the same thing as saying 'believed on him personally'. John wrote his gospel so many might 'have life in his name' which meant that they might 'have life in him'. God's name was to be holy and hallowed as God himself was holy and hallowed. When we call on the name of the Lord, we call on the Lord himself and when we are baptized in his name, we are baptized into him and the fellowship of his Church. He promised his followers that 'whatever you ask in my name, I will do it', suggesting that such a prayer would be in keeping with his divine nature as well as his teachings to his disciples. The apostles early preached that 'there was no other name given under heaven whereby men might be saved' except the name of Jesus, the character and ministry and personality of the risen Lord and Saviour. Paul wrote to the Philippians, stating that 'Therefore God hath highly exalted him and bestowed on him the name that is above every name; that at the name of Jesus every knee should bow in heaven and on earth and every tongue confess that Jesus Christ is Lord to the glory of God the father'."

Out of her own experience as well as her study of the Bible, Lydia Baxter, in 1870, her sixty-first year, wrote a poem which William H. Doane has set to music, giving the Christian world its finest gospel song on "The Name of Jesus". Her poem began:

Take the name of Jesus with you, Child of sorrow and of woe;
It will joy and comfort give you; Take it then where'er you go.
Precious name, O how sweet! Hope of earth and joy of heaven!

In her poem, His Name was shield against every foe, a source
of constant, abiding joy and the guarantee of everlasting life in
heaven. While some of the names we bear are names that divide
us, others are names that unite us. And the name above every
name to unite all God's sheep into one sheepfold is the name of
Jesus. Lydia Baxter wrote many other poems that became gospel
songs, "There is a gate that stands ajar" ranking second to "Take
the name of Jesus with you," but if she had penned but that one
poem, and Doane had composed but that one tune, they would
have been worthy of the place their gospel song has earned for
itself in the hearts and hymnals of Christians the world over.

33.

TAKE TIME TO BE HOLY

A sermon *and* song inspired a sixty year old Englishman to
write a hymn that has become a sermon *in* song. The sermon
was actually two sermons in one, delivered by two different men
on two different occasions in two different places and on two
different themes. But since they supplemented each other in the
mind and heart of one eager listener, William Dunn Longstaff,
they may well have been one and the same.

The first half of the double barrel sermon was delivered in a
Church at New Brighton, England, probably during the next to
the last decade of the nineteenth century by a clergyman whose
name has either been lost or forgotten. But both his text and
his exposition burned themselves deeply into the heart of listener
Longstaff, a wealthy and devout philanthropist of Sunderland,
England, whose financial independence resulted from the superb
wooden ships which his father built during the days when Britan-
nia ruled the waves. The well-to-do business man recalled that

the preacher said, "My text is found in 1 Peter 1:16, 'Be ye holy, for I am holy'. If you will turn in your Bibles to the Old Testament, and read Leviticus 11:44, you will find the words which St. Peter quoted in his first letter in the New Testament. For the writer of the third Book of Moses said these words in that passage, 'For I am the Lord your God; consecrate yourselves, therefore, and be holy, for I am holy'. The forty-fifth verse concludes with the very same admonition, couched in these words, 'For I am the Lord who brought you up out of the land of Egypt, to be your God: you shall therefore be holy, for I am holy'." Thus was the doctrine of Scriptural holiness brought to the attention of William Longstaff (1822-1894).

The more he thought about it, the more logical and practical it became, and soon he was regarding the idea of holiness not as an appendage to the gospel, but as the heart of it all and considering the Methodist emphasis on holiness not as an abnormal thing, but as the normal result of Christian growth. Thus he deplored the extremes to which some sects went in preaching and practicing their false conceptions of holiness and which led them to emotional excesses entirely out of keeping with true Christian doctrine and living.

"Since holiness is the life of God in the life of man, surely we need not scream and shout as if God were deaf, nor make fools of ourselves in our services of public worship as if God Himself were a fool," he asserted. "We are not to be holy as idiots are holy, or as drunkards and fools are holy," he stated, "but we are to be holy as God Himself is holy", and he longed to exhibit in his own life that quality of holiness about which he preached and spoke so fervently.

It was not until a returned missionary to China addressed a conference of Christian people at Keswick, England some time later than Longstaff linked together in his own mind the idea of holiness with the Christian conception of time. For when Dr. Griffith John used the phrase "Take time and be holy" in his address, something clicked in Longstaff's subconscious, and he substituted for the three-letter word "and" the two-letter word "to", making the phrase "Take time to be holy" his very own. Before he knew it, the words and phrases were becoming lines and stanzas, and he was reading the first stanza of his own original hymn:

Take time to be holy, Speak oft with thy Lord;
Abide in him always, And feed on His word;
Make friends of God's children, Help those who are weak,
Forgetting in nothing, His blessing to seek.

When he thought of those frantic people who rushed hither and yon trying to force God to do their own will instead of sitting down so God could reveal unto them His will, he wrote these words:

Take time to be holy, Let Him be thy guide;
And run not before Him, whatever betide.
In joy or in sorrow, Still follow the Lord,
And, looking to Jesus, Still trust in his word.

When the four stanzas were finally complete, the poet was about as much surprised as anyone else at the beauty and simplicity of his composition. And there the story would have ended had it not been for the fact that a minister questioned the propriety of permitting a soloist to sing in his Church, regardless of the fame or vocal skill or Christian consecration of the singer. When Dwight L. Moody and his distinguished singer, Ira D. Sankey, went to England for the purpose of conducting evangelistic services in the Churches of the island kingdom, Rev. Arthur A. Rees, the founder and pastor of Bethesda Chapel in Sunderland, was perfectly willing to welcome Moody as a preacher, but had some qualms of conscience about including Sankey, the singer. "Some of my people," he explained to the two Americans, "regard the pipe organ as 'the devil's box of whistles' and consequently they rule out instruments and solos. They insist that God can be praised only by congregational singing, even if that singing is of the poorest possible sort." When some who had been spiritually stirred by Sankey's singing suggested that the pastor, in all fairness, owed it to the musician to hear him sing what they called "a trial solo", Rees could hardly decline.

So the English clergyman and the American singer met in the home of William Longstaff, then the treasurer of Bethesda Chapel, to undergo the minister's scrutiny and try to convince him that God could sing through Sankey as well as preach through Moody. Sankey sat at Longstaff's harmonium and, accompanying himself in a style peculiar to his own genius, "passed his examination with high honors." Thus did Bethesda Chapel become the second Church in England to invite the famous team to conduct special services within its walls.

It was during this engagement than Sankey discovered Longstaff's poem, and insisted on having a copy made for his own use. Following his own advice, Longstaff continued not only to "take time to be holy" but also to "make time to be holy", and enriched with the quality of his devotion to the Lord all who came within the radiance of his influence.

Later he spoke of his close friendship with Moody and Sankey in the highest terms, and was little surprised when "Take time to be holy" was included in the 1891 edition of Sankey's book "Gospel Hymns and Sacred Songs and Solos", coupled with the hymntune entitled "Holiness" which George Stebbins had composed the previous year. From Sankey's files, the words had found their way into the columns of several religious journals. When a friend clipped a copy for Stebbins, the composer placed it among his other papers, setting them to music while in India assisting Dr. George Pentecost and Bishop Thoburn in a series of evangelistic services.

So England, America, China and India had a hand in giving the words and music of "Take time to be holy" to the Christian world. If the devout believers in these four strategic lands would heed more carefully the advice and admonitions contained in the four stanzas of this hymn, the tensions between them would relax and the bonds of friendship and love grow stronger and stronger.

34.

THE CHRISTIAN'S GOODNIGHT

Devotees of other religions may chant and cry at the funeral services of the departed, but Christians alone can sing. And there is a vast difference between the wailing cry of a non-Christian at the final services preceeding burial or cremation, and the confident song of triumph with which the loved ones of departed saints herald their arrival over on the other shore!

While those to whom the other world is shrouded in mystery beat their breasts and scream their defiance at "whatever gods there be" over on the other side of death, Christians recall the words of the Master, who said "In my father's house are many mansions; if it were not so, I would have told you. I go to prepare a place for you and if I go and prepare a place for you, I will come again and receive you unto myself that where I am there ye may be also."

At the funeral services of believers, the familiar verses of Psalm Twenty-three are read, with their reminder that "I shall dwell in the house of the Lord forever". Thus, when a Christian dies, those who stand at the bedside cannot say "Goodbye", or even whisper a pious "Farewell". The soul so soon to return to the Creator who fashioned us all in his own image, is not to be forever destroyed, for the grave is not the end of everything. Death is never a dead end street or a blind alley, but a tunnel, through which one passes to find the light of the glory of God bursting in all its radiance in the heavenly places where Christ Jesus dwells and reigns forever more.

In that spirit, the greatest hymn writer in the history of the Christian Church, Rev. Charles Wesley, passed from this life on May 29, 1788, at the advanced age of eighty-one. The last hymn that fell from the lips of him who had sung more than 6,500 hymns in fifty years, was dictated to the preacher-poet's wife a few days prior to his death, and consisted of these lines:

In age and feebleness extreme, Who shall a sinful worm redeem:
Jesus my only joy thou art, Strength of my failing flesh and heart:
Oh, could I catch a smile from thee And drop into eternity!

To a Christian, death is always a dropping into eternity! This concept is nowhere more graphically seen than in the passing of Rev. John Harper enroute from England to America on the ill-fated Titanic, to accept the pastorate of a great Church in Chicago. As the "unsinkable" vessel, ripped by an iceberg, slowly settled to the bottom of the Atlantic, Harper swam among those so soon to be claimed by a watery grave, telling them to "Believe on the Lord Jesus Christ and thou shalt be saved". One survivor told how he watched until he noticed that the preacher's strength was almost gone. Then, sinking down into the depths, Harper cried aloud "I am going down —" only to shout a moment later — "No, I am going up!" and then he disappeared from sight.

Sarah Doudney had been taught very early in life that a Christian never feared death, but rather, embraced death as a gift from God. While her childish mind could not comprehend those words, she remembered them, and, as she grew older, began to see in them the confident faith that sustained many in their hours of sorrow and loss. Her poetic gifts were natural ones, needing little cultivation to bring them to fruition. When she was looking through an old family scrapbook one rainy afternoon, she chanced upon a picture of an old grist-mill, with this line underneath the picture, "The mill cannot grind with the water that has passed". The fifteen year old girl picked up a pencil and a piece of paper, and before the day ended she had written the words of a poem "The Lessons of the Water-mill", which, when set to music, became one of the popular favorites of the day, not only in her native Britain but also in the United States.

Miss Doudney, born near Portsmouth, England, moved at a very early age to a remote village in Hampshire, where she was destined to spend most of the remaining years of her life. The rural atmosphere provided her with just the opportunity and inspiration she needed to develop her talent for writing, and soon she was earning a reputation as a prolific writer of hymns, poems, songs and stories. The death of a very dear friend early in 1871 reminded the sensitive young woman that the Christians of the early centuries always said "Goodnight" to their dying loved ones, since they were so certain of their awakening on the Resurrection Morning. That thought haunted her for many days following her friend's funeral and burial, and, when she could not discover any comforting hymn or sacred poem on that theme, she decided to write one herself.

That very same year, Rev. John Ellerton (1826-1893) was to write the majestic stanzas of his hymn:

Now the laborer's task is o'er, Now the battle day is past,
Now upon the farther shore, Lands the voyager at last.
Father, in thy gracious keeping Leave we now thy servant
   sleeping.

In somewhat the same pattern, Miss Doudney later wrote her hymn "Saviour, when the day is ending", with its beautiful refrain at the close of each stanza, "Set thy seal on every heart, Jesus, bless us ere we part". But this time she took as her theme the ancient Christian custom of bidding dying believers "Goodnight", and wrote the seven stanzas of one of her finest poems, "The Christian's Goodnight". Some of her stanzas contained these lines:

Sleep on, beloved, Sleep and take thy rest,
Lay down thy head upon thy Saviour's breast;
We love thee well, but Jesus loved thee best — Goodnight.
Until the Easter glory lights the skies, Until the dead in Jesus
   shall arise,
And he shall come — but not in lowly guise — Goodnight.
Until made beautiful by love divine,
Thou, in the likeness of thy Lord shalt shine,
And he shall bring that golden crown of thine — Goodnight.
Only "Goodnight" beloved, not "Farewell"!
A little while and all his saints shall dwell
In hallowed union, indivisible — Goodnight.

The singer-composer Ira D. Sankey, who set Elizabeth Clephane's "The Ninety and Nine" to music, discovered this poem while on an evangelistic tour of the British isles with Dwight L.

Moody, and gave it an original musical setting, thus giving to Christendom another hymn on heaven from the pen of a devout and consecrated Christian woman.

While another talented English poet, Anna Laetitia Barbauld (1743-1825) had once said, "Say not Goodnight, but in some brighter sphere bid me Goodmorning", Sarah Doudney took the word with which first century Christians bade their comrades farewell and translated it into a noble hymn, with an insistent note of assurance in the life everlasting, and with the Christian confidence that believers, after death, are forever with the Lord.

35.

THE HOME OF THE SOUL

"Was Mr. Bunyan in jail when he wrote that, Daddy?" the little lad asked his father.

"Yes, son, he was. But it wasn't the first time the great preacher had been imprisoned, but the third," the father, Philip Phillips, replied.

"You mean he was put in jail three times?" the boy asked.

"Three times," his father answered.

"Why?" the lad continued. "He wasn't a crook, was he?"

Philips smiled. "No, son, he was one of the most brilliant men of his day. But he was put in jail because the King of England refused to let men like John Bunyan preach without a permit, and he didn't give him a permit when Bunyan asked for it, so he went ahead and preached anyway, and was arrested and put into prison for breaking the law."

"Do you have to have a permit to sing, Daddy?"

"Oh, no," Phillips explained. "This is the United States of America and here we enjoy freedom of religion, and no one has to get a permit from any kind of government official to preach the gospel like some men do, or sing it like I do."

"Didn't you sing for the king once, Daddy?" the boy asked again.

"Not the king, son. We don't have kings here in America. But I did sing for the president, whose name was Abraham Lincoln."

"Did he like your song?"

"He must have, because he asked me to sing it again at the close of the meeting," Phillips explained.

"Which song was it, Daddy?"

"I sang Mrs. Ellen Gates' Song, 'Your Mission'," Phillips replied.

"She's the woman you asked to write that new hymn, isn't she?"

"Yes she is," the older man said. "In fact, her letter came just this morning, and I am curious to know what she wrote. You see, I asked her to write a new hymn based upon these words from Bunyan's famous book 'Pilgrim's Progress', and that was the reason I was reading the passage to you a moment ago. I wanted to see what Bunyan had in mind so we can compare his prose with Mrs. Gates' poetry."

Picking up a copy of the famous allegory, Mr. Phillips read aloud the closing portions of the story, in which the two characters Christian and Hopeful are about to enter into the Celestial City. "Now I saw in my dream that these two men went in at the gate; and lo, as they entered, they were transfigured; and they had raiment put on them that shone like gold. There were also those that met them with harps and crowns and gave them to them; the harps to praise withal and the crowns in token of honor. Then I heard in my dream that all the bells in the city rang again for joy, and it was said unto them, Enter ye into the joy of your Lord. Now just as the gates were opened to let in the men, I looked in after them and behold, the city shone like the sun; the streets also were paved with gold and in them walked many men with crowns on their heads and palms in their hands and golden harps to sing praises withal."

When he paused to see the majestic imagery of it all in his mind's eye, Phillips' son said, "And he wrote all that in jail."

"Yes, my boy," the father added, "he wrote it when he was imprisoned in Bedford, England, for preaching as a Baptist minister without the approval of the King of England, back in 1675.

This was the part I sent to Mrs. Gates. Now, let us see what she has done with it."

Eagerly picking up the letter postmarked New York City, thirty-one year old Philip Phillips (1834-1895) opened it, took out the letter which he set to one side, and began to read the poem which Ellen Huntington Gates (1836-1920) had enclosed. His little son listened quietly as his father began to read:

> I will sing you a song of that beautiful land
> That far-away home of the soul,
> Where no storms ever beat on the glittering strand,
> While the years of eternity roll.
>
> O that home of the soul, In my visions and dreams
> Its bright, jasper walls I can see;
> Till I fancy but thinly the veil intervenes
> Between that fair city and me.

When he finished reading her four stanzas, Mr. Phillips was so deeply moved, that he immediately turned to the little organ in the room that fateful day in 1865, and, still balancing his little son on his knee, began picking out a melody for the new lines. Soon he was singing Mrs. Gates' new words to his new music, while the boy looked and listened in silence.

Following the custom of the day, the composer repeated the last two lines of each stanza in the form of a "chorus" or "refrain" writing his music in a rather odd style, using the four lines of each stanza, with three lines being repeated and added to the end, making a seven-line song out of the four-line original. But he captured the simple sincerity of the poem in the equally simple and moving mood of his music, little dreaming that the new song would one day be used at the funeral services of both father and son Phillips.

For, when the lad who sat on his father's knee in reverent silence during the composing of the tune, suddenly passed away, "The Home of the Soul" was sung at his funeral. And later, when the father who became not only an inspiring singer and composer but also a successful business man and publisher in Fredonia, New York, died, his close friend and associate, Ira D. Sankey, sang "The Home of the Soul" at his funeral. Strangely enough, the musician had said of his tune, "This hymn seems to have had God's special blessing upon it from the very beginning."

Just as Phillips had been moved to give more of his time and talent to the field of evangelistic singing by the success which attended his musical setting and public singing of Mrs. Gates' earlier poem "Your Mission", so he inspired, by his winsome personality, Ira D. Sankey to turn his back upon a lucrative career as a revenue officer and give himself and his musical talent to the service of God by following in Phillips' footsteps. That Sankey made a wise choice in following his friend's example may be seen in the fact that his musical settings of "The ninety and nine", "I'm praying for you" and dozens of other hymns and sacred songs are still high in favor in the hymnals of many Churches, and still reach deep down inside the hearts of both those who sing them and those who listen.

When Martin Luther wrote the Preface to his commentary on Paul's letter to the Romans, he little dreamed that a nameless layman would be reading his words one night several centuries later in a little prayer-meeting in London's tiny Aldersgate Street, when John Wesley would feel his "heart strangely warmed".

Nor did Ellen Huntington Gates dream of the spiritual chain-reaction that would result when she wrote "Your Mission" as a young lady of twenty-five, in 1860. But the blessings that bore fruit in the lives of Phillips and Sankey bear eloquent testimony to the fact that God's Providential Hand was still at work, and if her stanzas did no more than inspire "The home of the soul" and "The ninety and nine", they produced a harvest more beautiful than the planter of the seed ever dreamed possible.

36.

THE OLD TIME RELIGION

When William Steffe, a church musician and song-leader from Richmond, Virginia accepted an invitation to take charge of the music at a Georgia Camp Meeting back in 1855, he little dreamed that his visit to the state which General Oglethorpe had founded a century and a quarter before, would prove to be the most eventful trip of his life. For it was while he was in charge of the Camp Meeting music that he was inspired to write the words and music of a new gospel hymn, "Say brothers, will you meet us, On Canaan's happy shore". Taking a cue from the Negro spirituals, he repeated the first line of his new hymn three times before singing the last line, and, again following the pattern established by the unknown authors and composers of the Negro's sacred songs, he sang the words of his Chorus, "Glory, glory, hallelujah, For ever evermore", to the same music as the verse.

The success of his new gospel hymn was due to simplicity and repetition, both of which characterized the popular spirituals of his day. That Steffe made a grand success of his first original gospel hymn is attested by the fact that it was to his tune that Julia Ward Howe later wrote the stirring stanzas of her majestic poem, "The Battle Hymn of the Republic".

A little over thirty years after Steffe caught the mood of the spirituals and made it his own, young Rev. Charles D. Tillman (1861-1943) was assisting his Methodist evangelist father in a series of evangelistic services at Lexington, South Carolina, a few miles from the capitol city of Columbia. In the custom of the day a large tent was erected on the edge of town, and the members of the Churches as well as the non-members were invited to come and participate in the singing and listen to the preaching of the father and son team. Since the tent was only large enough to hold the white worshippers who crowded it to capacity, the Negro

Christians stayed in the background during the evening meetings.

However, the Tillmans always made it a practice to turn over their tent on Sunday afternoons to the colored people of the communities in which they conducted their revival services, and they came from far and near to fill the tent, and to stand arouund on the outside, singing and shouting their encouraging "Amens" and generally enjoying the inspiration such a gathering always affords. Charlie made it his practice to be on the outskirts of the crowd when those Sunday afternoon services were scheduled, because he never knew when he might get a good idea for a new gospel song, or hear the Negroes singing a spiritual he had never heard before.

Thus it came about that young Charlie was present that memorable Sunday afternoon in 1889 in Lexington, South Carolina, little dreaming that he was soon to hear a new spiritual with which his name would be associated from that day on. After he had heard the familiar strains of "Go Down, Moses", and the haunting lyrics of "Swing low, sweet chariot", and after the last note of "Little David, play on your harp", or "Oh, Mary, don't you weep, don't you mourn" had died away, he suddenly awakened to the fact that the colored poeple were singing something he had never heard before. Soon above the rythmic clapping of hundreds of pairs of hands, and the steady monotonous beat of dozens of pairs of feet, he managed to catch a line or two that sounded like:

Tis the old-time religion, tis the old-time religion;
Tis the old-time religion, And it's good enough for me.

He soon realized that those words comprised the chorus, while the stanzas were being sung to the very same melody, with the first line being repeated three times before the words "It's good enough for me", came in. He caught some phrases about the old-time religion being "good for the Hebrew children" and "tried in the fiery furnace", and was assured that it was also "good for Paul and Silas". Then, when they sang that it was "good for the prophet Daniel" yesterday as well as for every member of the family today, he knew that it could finally be guaranteed to "take us home to glory" when we laid our burdens down.

Charlie felt in his heart that the new song was a "natural" if he ever heard one, and could hardly wait for the meeting to close so he could corner one of the song leaders and get the words and music of the spiritual straight from headquarters. When the meeting finally terminated after what seemed like hours of preaching, singing, testifying and exhorting, young Tillman was introduced to a Negro blacksmith by the name of Rawlings, who seemed to be the self-appointed song leader for the group. At Charlie's invitation, the two men stepped over to a quiet spot underneath some shade trees beyond the confusion of the dispersing crowd and the youthful preacher-composer had the devout blacksmith sing the words and music over several times, while he jotted both down on the cleanest piece of paper he could find.

Rawlings had no idea where the song had originated since it had been sung by his people for years and years. Undoubtedly it had been created almost as spontaneously as "Swing low, sweet chariot" by some unnamed or unknown colored Christian, who felt that he was expressing the longings, desires and aspirations of his people as they emerged from the dark night of African paganism into the new light of the Christian faith. Strangely enough, after the Negro singer assisted the young Methodist song-leader in copying down the new song, the two men separated and their paths never crossed again this side of glory.

But Charlie knew that "The old-time religion" would catch on just as rapidly with the white people as with the black, and that his friends back in Atlanta would welcome it with even more enthusiasm than those who had been singing it when he heard it for the first time. He was justified in his expectations, for soon the camp meetings and revival services in and around Atlanta, Georgia, were ringing with the lilting strains of "The old-time religion".

Two years later, when the young Methodist was making up a new collection of original hymns and songs, he harmonized and copyrighted the new spiritual, but he never made a penny on it because he refused to charge anyone for its use. He always granted free permission for its inclusion in other hymnals and song books as requests came to him from all over the world.

Later, when the composer tried to sell one of his song books to the Board of Education of South Carolina, for use in the schools of that state, he learned that his book was adopted because in it he included the story of his discovery of "The old-time religion" just a few miles from the state's capitol city.

Tillman lived to celebrate his golden wedding anniversary on Christmas Eve, 1939, his four daughters joining with Charlie and his wife Anna to make the occasion a festive and memorable one in every way.

Before his death, he had edited and published twenty collections of hymns and songs, and confessed that he had lost count of the number of tunes he had been privileged to compose. His two most popular tunes, "Life's railway to heaven" and "My Mother's Bible" are characterized by the same simplicity as the music of the spiritual he popularized.

Collaborating with a Negro blacksmith named Rawlings, Tillman gave the Church "The old-time religion"; while he composed the music for his railroad song at the request of a Georgia Baptist minister, Rev. M. E. Abbey, and the tune for "My Mother's Bible" at the urging of another evangelist, Rev. M. B. Williams, with whom he was associated in a series of services in New York State in 1892.

Charlie not only sang about "the old-time religion", he lived it out in his own life, and that it was good enough to take him "home to glory" is the unanimous opinion of those who knew and loved him during his long and eventful life of eighty-two years.

37.

THE VICTORY MAY DEPEND ON YOU

George Orlia Webster (1866-1942) well knew what was involved when he chose to give his life to the Christian ministry. He knew the trials and tribulations of a clergyman's life as well as its joys and triumphs, because his father had been a pioneer Baptist minister in the North River and Indian Lake country of New York state in the last quarter of the nineteenth century, organizing and building several churches. Young George, however, served his early apprenticeship running logs down the Hudson River for one of the numerous lumber camps that dotted the north woods country, then working for a while in the Gore Mountain Garnet Mines. While this would hardly be considered adequate preparation for the pulpit, nevertheless, it gave the young man an insight into the lives of laboring people that stood him in good stead in the years of his active ministry.

To George Webster the Church was not a haven for "white-collar theologians" who were afraid to get their ministerial robes dirty in the muck and mire of everyday living. It was a challenge to a man who was not afraid to wear callouses on his hands as proud proof that he was earning his daily bread by the sweat of his own brow and the labor of his own hands.

Later in life, when the health of his family required that he return to the country as a tiller of the soil, Webster went to a farm near Glens Falls, New York, where he lived for some years. However, his interest in cultivating men's souls as well as God's soil led him to serve and build up several struggling congregations in the surrounding territory, some of which are now included in the Larger Parish of the Glens Falls Presbyterian Church.

After finishing his schooling at Vermont Academy, at Saxon's River, Vermont, his "trial sermon" must have met with enthusiastic approval, for shortly thereafter he was licensed to preach by

143

the Baptist Church in North River, New York. Saxon's River Baptist Church also granted him a license to preach, but it was in the Baptist Church at Mount Pelier, Vermont that he was finally ordained in 1892, at the age of twenty-six.

The ability to make rhymes almost without conscious effort must have been born into George O. Webster, because, very early in life, he began to write the poems he was to continue writing with effortless ease until his death in 1942. During his pastorates in Vermont, New Hampshire, and New York, he continued his regular output of religious verse on a wide variety of subjects and in many and varied metrical patterns and before he laid his pen down for the last time, more than two-thousand hymns and songs had poured from his fluent pen, from the overflow of his consecrated heart.

When he was away from home attending a Conference for Sunday School workers in Cincinnati, Ohio, and scheduled to give the keynote address to church school representatives from all over the state, he found himself a bit on edge a few hours before he was to deliver the principal speech of the evening. He retired to his room for prayer and meditation, in order to get hold of himself as well as to go over the matters he intended to include in his talk. While thinking about the material he had prepared to share with the delegates to the state-wide conference, and his own slight nervousness at the thought of standing before so many strangers, trying to attract their interest and sympathy as well as attempting to win them over to his own personal point of view, the thought suddenly came to him that the victory that night would not depend upon anything else or anyone else but himself. It was almost as if he had heard a voice saying, "The victory may depend on you". In a moment he was alive and yet calm, as he began to jot down some stanzas that seemed to be crowding into his heart and mind.

"Through the land a call is sounding, And it comes to age and
    youth;
Tis a summons to the conflict, In the cause of right and truth;
To the standard of our Captain, Lo, there comes a faithful few;
But the victory, my brother, may depend on you.

Chorus: The victory may depend on you, The victory may de-
    pend on you;

144

Dare to stand among the few, With the faithful tried
    and true,
For the victory may depend on you."

Enroute to the scene of the Conference, he showed his three stanzas and chorus to Mr. J. H. Fillmore whom he chanced to meet on the way. Fillmore was elated, and immediately composed a new tune for Webster's new lines, introducing the new song at one of the sessions of the conference the very next day. It made a profound impression upon the delegates, who carried the new song back to their homes and churches, teaching it everywhere they went. Copyrighted in 1906, the song soon found its place in the collections of gospel songs being used in many churches throughout the English speaking world, a musical interpretation of Psalm 98:1, "O sing unto the Lord a new song, for he has done marvelous things; his right hand and his holy arm hath gotten him the victory", and I John 5:4, "This is the victory that overcometh the world, even our faith".

In the same spontaneous spirit, Webster dashed off the lines of the gospel song "If Christ should come to me", writing them down on an old envelope propped against a freight car, after jogging to town in an old lumber wagon to get a load of "smelly commercial fertilizer" for his farm.

When he was confined to the hospital in Plattsburg, New York waiting to learn whether or not an injured foot would have to be amputated, his music publisher and friend, Mr. G. G. Tullar, suggested that he write a song a day to help pass the time away. The day he waited to hear the good news that he would not have to lose his limb, he wrote the stanzas of the gospel hymn "Skies will soon be blue".

It was during my father's pastorate at the Presbyterian Church in Fort Edward, New York, 1913-1918, that he and Webster became fast friends, collaborating on many hymns and songs, Webster writing the stanzas and father, Rev. S. K. Emurian, composing the music. While father was writing "The Smile Song" (Smile whenever you can) that was to be sung by thousands of American soldiers during the dark days prior to and during the first World War, Webster was writing "Men of our America" that became popular in Men's and YMCA gatherings and conferences and "Your flag and my flag", a song that sold over three million copies during those same years.

His gospel hymn "I Need Jesus" written during his long pastorate at the Federated Church, Essex, New York, became the most popular one he was ever privileged to write. The spirit that characterized his life and ministry is embodied in the stanzas of his last hymn "Jesus my Saviour" written in 1941, the year prior to his death.

Jesus, my Saviour, Master and Friend, Loving and tender, Strong to defend,
Comforter Holy, Teacher and Guide, Keep me, I pray thee, close to thy side.
Mighty defender, Saviour so tender, Thee would I render, Holiest praise.

38.

WHEN THE ROLL IS CALLED UP YONDER

When the forty-four Bishops of the Methodist Episcopal Church (as the northern branch of American Methodism was known prior to the union of the Methodist Episcopal Church, the Methodist Episcopal Church, South, and the Methodist Protestant Church in 1939) met to appoint a committee of eleven representative clergymen and laymen of the Church to cooperate with a similar committee from the southern Church, in producing a new edition of The Methodist Hymnal, scheduled for publication in 1905, one of the laymen chosen was James Milton Black (1856-1938) a distinguished citizen, musician and composer of Williamsport, Pennsylvania.

Professor Black, as he was affectionately called in his home town, had moved to Pennsylvania from Grahamsville, Sullivan County, New York, in 1882 and had made quite a name for himself as a gospel worker, a Churchman, a musician and composer of hymns and sacred songs. As a member of Williamsport's Pine Street Methodist Church, he interested himself in the worship and work of Methodism with the enthusiasm which characterized most of his endeavors during his long and fruitful life of eighty-two years. The importance of his appointment to this Hymn Book Commission may be seen in the fact that it was the first joint effort on the part of the northern and southern branches of the Church since their tragic division many years prior to the Civil War. Furthermore, from a collection of 2,217 acceptable hymns and songs, the twenty-two commission members had to select 748 for the new hymnal, a difficult and, at times, a very trying task. Black was not a novice, however, because the first song book he ever edited, "Songs of the Soul, Numbers 1 and 2" sold more than a million copies. Two years after that initial success a half-million copies of his "Chorus of Praise" were published, that soon being followed by another musical success "Praise and Promise" in which he collaborated with Bishop C. C. Mc-Cabe (the man who introduced "The Battle Hymn of the Republic" to the nation following his imprisonment in Libby Prison during the Civil War). "Epworth Hymnal Number 3" and "Songs of faith and hope" enjoyed the same prominence in later years.

As a composer, Black had the rare gift of picking out melodies and tunes that caught the popular ear, and, of the more than one-thousand tunes that came from his fluent pen, hundreds were in common usage during the composer's lifetime. His most popular song, however, was one that would hardly have met the stiff requirements of the Hymnal Committee, because technically it was not a hymn at all, but merely a good gospel song. And not being a hymn, it would hardly have been included among the 748 chosen for the 1905 edition of The Methodist Hymnal. Nevertheless, it became universally popular, and was translated into dozens of foreign tongues, being sung not only in English speaking churches throughout Christendom but also at many roll calls in the United States Army, at home and abroad. For many years, Mr. Black kept the secret of the song to himself, only revealing it at the insistent request of a reporter for a weekly newspaper magazine "Grit" in the hope that it might bring those outside the Church into the fellowship of the Kingdom of God.

One day, while walking through an alley not far from his home at the corner of Market and Front Streets in Williamsport, the composer saw a little girl sitting on the front porch of a very dilapitated looking house. From her appearance, her ragged clothes and torn shoes, he knew her to be very poor. As she turned, he recognized her as a member of a family of which he had heard, the daughter of a drunken father and a mother who was forced to take in sewing and washing in order to provide for her little ones. He figured her to be about thirteen years old, and was impressed by her pretty light hair and soft blue eyes. Calling her by name, Mr. Black asked if she would like to come to Sunday School the following Sunday morning. A wistful expression crept into the girl's eyes, while the suspicion of a tear could be seen on her lashes. Looking up with a crimson face, she said, "Yes, I would like to go, but —", to which the composer replied, "All right, Bessie; I understand." The next day a new dress, shoes, hat and other things dear to her heart found their way to the girl's home, and a week later, when Black made it his business to pass that way again and ask Bessie if she would like to come to Sunday School, she replied gratefully, "Yes, indeed."

She not only showed up the following Sunday but every Sunday after that for many weeks, finally joining one of the societies in the Church and becoming a very faithful worker. Having known nothing but misery and poverty for many years, the new life she discovered in the fellowship of the Church became the brightest spot in her life, and, at every regular meeting, she was always found in her accustomed place. One night the roll was being called, each member responding with an original expression or some Biblical quotation. As each name was called, the members responded until the ninety-ninth name was reached. When the secretary called the name "Bessie", there was no response. Again her name was called and again there was no answer. Thinking she had not heard her name, Mr. Black rose and repeated it for the third time, but again everything was as still as death and not a person stirred or spoke. In that moment, the musician had a strange presentiment. "What if this girl should never answer again?" he thought. "What if she should die? What, if, when the final summons came, she would fail to answer?" These thoughts flashed through his mind in an instant.

Looking through the Hymnal to find some hymn or song that would fit the occasion, he was unable to discover anything suitable. Walking home after the meeting he thought of the incident, trifling as it was in one respect, but so solemn in another. As he entered the front door of his home the thought struck him anew, "What if she should never answer?" Almost unconsciously he blurted out these words:

When the trumpet of the Lord shall sound, and time shall be no
    more,
And the morning breaks eternal bright and fair;
When the saved of earth shall gather over on the other shore
And the roll is called up yonder, I'll be there.

No sooner had he said the words than his trained ear told him that he had something euphonious and, going immediately to his piano, he struck up the music almost as spontaneously as he had the words. In a remarkably short time he had finished the hymn, of which not a single word or note has been changed since that memorable night.

Later, to his dismay, he learned from his friends that Bessie had indeed been sick that night, with an illness so serious that a few days later it claimed her life. Because of this personal connection with the authorship of the gospel song, the poet-composer was reluctant for many years to share the story of its origin with the world. He credited its popularity to the fact that he felt it was literally forced out of him that historic night.

Mr. Black became one of Williamsport's most famous citizens, making his home, at 325 Park Avenue in that city until his death in a local hospital on Wednesday, December 17, 1938, at the age of eighty-two, following an operation he had undergone the previous morning. His obituary contained these lines, "He was a 32nd degree Mason and a member of the Pine Street Methodist Church. While he had been retired for a number of years, he formerly had been in the insurance business — Interment will be made in Wildwood Cemetery. The Rev. Dr. J. Howard Ake will officiate."

Nearly twenty years later, Rev. Frank W. Ake, a son of the officiating clergyman, was appointed Pastor of Pine Street Church.

The writer is indebted to the Reference Librarian of the James V. Brown Library, Williamsport, Pennsylvania, Miss Catherine

T. Shulenberger, for providing him with the information contained in this story. No finer conclusion could be written, to this narrative than to quote the closing lines of James M. Black's finest song, lines he lived out in his own life:

Let us labor for the Master from the dawn till setting sun;
Let us talk of all His wondrous love and care;
Then when all of life is over and our work on earth is done,
And the roll is called up yonder, I'll be there.

39.

WHEN THEY RING THE GOLDEN BELLS
FOR YOU AND ME

Daniel A. DeMarbelle spoke of himself as a "cute, curious, comical cuss" but that personal opinion was not shared by those who knew, respected, admired and loved him, for a more versatile and unusual man would be almost impossible to find. Born in Seville, France on the Fourth of July, 1818, DeMarbelle embarked upon a life of such variety that the variety itself became rather monotonous. While according to the old saying, a "rolling stone gathers no moss", it surely picks up a lot of experience, and in his travels to the far corners of the globe, DeMarbelle absorbed his share. His early love for wandering far from home led the roving youth to sign up with a whaling crew and spend several hectic years braving the perils of the Arctic seas, fighting with whales who refused to die and icebergs that refused to melt. When he got his fill of the frozen northland, he left the whaling crew and enlisted in the United States Navy during the Mexican War of 1847.

Having seen life to the south of him as well as to the north, he settled in between, abandoned the trade of seaman and sailor, and joined up with an American travelling opera company, filling the double role of musician and actor. When he wasn't playing for someone else to sing, he was singing while somebody else played. The lure of the footlights finally got the best of him, and he devoted most of his remaining years to stages and circuses. When he wasn't under the big top, thrilling a bunch of noisy kids with his antics as a circus clown, he was inside an auditorium or standing in the protective shade of a band shell, directing a group of carefree musicians or ham-actors to the delight of all who came within sight and sound of the show.

During the War Between the States, 1861-1865, DeMarbelle enlisted and served as a musician with the Sixth Michigan Infantry regiment. When he stayed in any particular place long enough to get acquainted with the townspeople, he could be found singing in the Methodist Church choir of a Sunday morning, and entertaining the courting couples in the park in the cool of an evening, regaling them, as well as the little kids, with his true or contrived stories about whaling expeditions to the north and Mexican adventures to the south, until he had them all hanging on every word, and hungering for more when the dramatic narratives finally came to an end.

Following the cessation of hostilities at Appomattox, when Confederate General Lee surrendered his Army of Northern Virginia to the Yankee leader, General Grant, DeMarbelle looked around for new worlds of entertainment to conquer, and soon organized a travelling troupe of fellow actors and booked his variety show throughout several northern states, headquartering in Detroit, Michigan. When showman Bailey (who was later to team up with "There's a fool born every minute" P. T. Barnum, to organize the Barnum and Bailey Circus), got together his first circus, he selected Daniel A. DeMarbelle, as his professional clown.

DeMarbelle, whose first name had been contracted by this time to "Dion", liked the work so much that he soon resigned from Bailey's employ and organized a circus of his own. He was enjoying unusual success in this new venture until the tragic day when flames levelled the show up in Canada and he lost everything he had. But showmen always know where to go to meet another of their kind, and it wasn't long before the versatile Frenchman had struck up an acquaintance with Colonel William

F. Cody, known familiarly as "Buffalo Bill", and been hired as an assistant in Cody's world-famous Wild West Troupe. The close friendship between the two showmen that resulted lasted until DeMarbelle's death in 1903.

It was during these years that Dion began to write verses for his own shows as well as for those who employed him to work in their circus or stage productions, and before long, he was revealing himself as an apt poet on almost every conceivable subject, from sacred songs to secular and ribald verse. Those who served with him during the Civil War carried many of his ditties back to their homes and taught others to sing the lilting and somewhat "corny" stuff their regimental poet had dashed off to while away the time or to encourage many a startled youth on the eve of his first battle.

One of those songs that became quite popular was entitled "We drank from the same canteen", and contained these lines:

> Sometimes it was water, Sometimes it was milk;
> Sometimes it was applejack, Finer than silk;
> But we drank from the same canteen!

At the opposite extreme, DeMarbelle revealed his finer feelings in a funeral hymn that also enjoyed widespread popularity before the turn of the century, "Over the dark and silent river." So the clown and entertainer became a poet and versifier, as well as a musician, composer, printer, woodcarver, magician and ventriloquist, until as a "one man show" he was a welcome visitor whereever he went.

Through the courtesy of Kendall White of the Elgin, Illinois "Courier-News", the story of DeMarbelle came to this writer's attention, and from clippings loaned by the newspaperman, the account of the writing of his most popular gospel song was brought to light. In 1887, while living in Kirkland, Illinois, where he organized and directed the Kirkland Brass Band for some years, DeMarbelle was inspired to pen the words and music of the gospel song with which his name will be forever associated, the one that became his only claim to fame.

At the age of sixty-nine, when most men are anticipating retirement and rest, DeMarbelle weary of this world, looked beyond this vale of tears and longed to hear the golden bells of the new Jerusalem ringing in his ears, a sound that was to be denied him for sixteen heart-breaking, empty and lonely years until his death at the age of eighty-five. Soon he was teaching his friends his new song, and they were joining him in the first stanza:

There's a land beyond the river that we call the sweet forever,
And we only reach that shore by faith's decree;
One by one we gain the portals There to dwell with the immortals,
When they ring the golden bells for you and me.

His biographer, Attorney James M. Huff of Belvidere, Illinois, who looked for two years before locating DeMarbelle's grave in the Bluff City Cemetery, said the popularity of this gospel song is due to the fact that "we all become partners in the democracy of death".

When he learned that the poet lived for a while in an abandoned school house in Wayne, Illinois, and had been buried by the G.A.R. (Grand Army of the Republic) after his death in Sherman Hospital, December 18, 1903, and that the only marker above the poet's final resting place was a typical $6 government stone, bearing only the inscription "Drum Major D. A. DeMarbelle, 6th Mich Inf", Huff urged the heirs of the boys of Company E, immortalized by the writer in a poem entitled "To The Elgin Boys", to place a more appropriate stone above DeMarbelle's grave. Then it was that the interested lawyer discovered that the talented genius from France had never received a penny of royalty for all his poems and songs, and spent his last years in tragic poverty. But for the kindness of a man named Smith Wyllys, who gave him a furnished room over his blacksmith shop, DeMarbelle would have had nowhere to lay his head, and but for the benevolence of J. D. Morris, who fed him free of charge at the Morris Hotel, he would have starved to death.

"He gave us his poems and songs," Huff wrote, "and we gave him forgetfulness in return." While the many popular ballads DeMarbelle wrote have long since been forgotten, this one in which he expressed his "longing for eternal life" will live in the hearts of Christian people, because of the simplicity and sincerity which characterize both its words and music.

So the spirit of Daniel A. DeMarbelle (1818-1903) lives on, and the man who was praised as a Shakesperean actor, applauded as an orator, laughed at as a clown, commended as a musician who could play almost every musical instrument, invited to be a Church soloist on Sunday morning and urged to call the figures at the community square dance the following night, will be remembered for the fact that the title of one of his songs "The sun may shine tomorrow" came true for him when he heard the ringing of "the golden bells" for which he had waited so eagerly and so long.

40.

YOUR MISSION

A snow-storm inspired the writing of this popular song and a meeting in the Senate chamber popularized it, but its success came in no way as a surprise or a shock to the author, Elizabeth Huntington Gates, because, when she finished her poem that dreary afternoon in 1860, she wrote, "Somehow I had a presentiment that it had wings and would fly into sorrowful hearts, uplifting and strengthening them".

Falling snow has inspired many a greater and lesser poet to rhymes and rhapsodies, but most of their works are descriptive or contemplative bits of verse in praise of the beauty, mystery and majesty of a snowfall. It wasn't in this spirit that twenty-five year old Ellen Gates (1835-1920) picked up her pen that fateful afternoon. To tell the truth, she was a bit peeved almost to the point of anger when she saw the snow begin to come down. After all, she had made her plans for the day, and those plans did not include a sleigh ride or a walk through a blinding snowstorm. And, to one in that rather rebellious mood, such a demonstration of the Creator's silent skill is not greeted with an enthusiastic welcome. But, as she watched the snow flakes gently piling up one atop the other, her mood gradually changed from open rebellion to calm resignation, and from accusing God of interfering with her plans to an acceptance of what God was doing in spite of the inconvenience to which it subjected her.

"If I cannot go out," she thought, "then I can stay in." And while that was far from a profound observation, it soon led her to a related idea, and she was saying to herself, "If I can't cross the ocean, then I can stay on the shore and help launch the ships that can; and if I cannot fight like Napoleon or Lord Nelson, then I can bind up the wounds of the soldiers and sailors, and be a Florence Nightingale instead. If I cannot reap the grain in the rich fields of Boaz, I can glean in the corners like Ruth, and if I have neither silver nor gold, like Peter and John, I can reach out my hand and raise up the fallen as Peter did when he cured the lame man of his infirmity at the gate of the Temple in Jerusalem. If I cannot give half my goods to feed the poor as did Zacchaeus when Jesus visited him in his home in Jericho, I can put in my 'widow's mite' with the knowledge that God looks upon the heart and accepts every gift given in the right spirit."

Suddenly, the snow that had intervened between Ellen Gates and her activities for the day, became not a wall that separated her from something she wanted to do, but a door through which she could enter into some new and unscheduled activity. She smiled to herself and said, "Maybe God knew what he was doing when he caused it to snow today," and for that reason she felt a strange "presentiment" as she picked up her slate and began to write:

If you cannot on the ocean Sail among the swiftest fleet,
Rocking on the highest billow, Laughing at the storms you meet,
You can stand among the sailors Anchored yet within the bay,
You can lend a hand to help them As they launch their boats
   away.

Before she knew it, she had written six stanzas, the last of which contained these lines:

Do not, then, stand idly waiting, For some greater work to do;
Fortune is a lazy goddess, She will never come to you.
Go and toil in any vineyard; Do not fear to do or dare;
If you want a field of labor, You can find it anywhere.

Then, in a moment of high inspiration, she fell on her knees and dedicated her new poem to God, asking him to consecrate it with his Divine blessing. Later she sent copies to several newspapers and magazines, where it was printed during the next few months.

Ellen Huntington Gates, who was born in 1835 in Torrington, Connecticut, and was identified by many as the sister of the well-known financial wizard, Collis P. Huntington, lived to see the day when he was pointed out as the brother of the brilliant author of "Your Mission".

The "Singing Pilgrim" Philip Phillips (1834-1895) spotted these stanzas in a New York newspaper, sensed their possibilities and set them to music, little dreaming that one day he would be singing them for the President of the United States.

When a meeting of United States Christian Commission was to convene in February 1865 in the Senate Chamber of the Capitol in Washington, D. C. the president of the Commission, Secretary Seward, invited the President of the United States, Abraham Lincoln, to be present. Lincoln, who was thrilled when he heard Chaplain C. C. McCabe sing "The Battle Hymn of the Republic" and requested a repeat performance, little expected to hear anything worth repeating at this particular gathering. However, when Mr. Phillips began singing "Your Mission" as a sacred solo, he sat up and took notice, and, as the singer finished the fifth stanza, the "Great Commoner" scribbled a note to Seward, "Let us have 'Your Mission' repeated." For Phillips had just sung these lines:

If you cannot in the conflict Prove yourself a soldier true,
If, where fire and smoke are thickest, There's no work for you to
    do,
When the battle-field is silent, You can go with careful tread,
You can bear away the wounded, You can cover up the dead.

Its popularity with the President assured its success with the people, and Mrs. Gates' "Presentiment" came true. Phillips was so deeply impressed by the response which the new song received that he later requested of the poet another sacred poem for which he planned to compose the tune. And the collaboration of the farm-boy musician and the rich city-girl poet resulted in one of the loveliest hymns ever written, "The home of the soul". Mrs. Gates' poem has sometimes been confused with, and mistaken for, a stanza of another hymn which Rev. Daniel March (1816-

1909) wrote in 1868. In the second stanza of his hymn "Hark! The voice of Jesus calling" March wrote:

If you cannot cross the ocean And the heathen lands explore,
You can find the heathen nearer, You can help them at your
    door.
If you cannot give your thousands, You can give the widow's
    mite
And the least you give for Jesus, Will be precious in his sight.

Strangely enough both hymns were written within the eight year period 1860-1868, and both earned a place in the hymnals of Christendom. But the poem penned by the talented wife of Isaac G. Gates is in a class all by itself for it had the rare distinction of having received the approval of the President of the United States. More important, though, is the fact that her hymn received the approval of her Heavenly Father, to whom the poet so early dedicated it, for, under His blessing, it has been a source of comfort and strength to many.